Thomas Schirrmacher (ed.)

The Humanisation of Slavery in the Old Testament

World of Theology Series

Published by the Theological Commission
of the World Evangelical Alliance

Volume 8

Thomas Schirrmacher (ed.)

The Humanisation of Slavery in the Old Testament

With a section on "The Role of Evangelicals in the Abolition of Slavery"

With contributions by David L. Baker and John Warwick Montgomery

With a Foreword by Thomas K. Johnson

Assisted by Ruth Baldwin

WIPF & STOCK · Eugene, Oregon

Wipf and Stock Publishers
199 W 8th Ave, Suite 3
Eugene, OR 97401

The Humanisation of Slavery in the Old Testament
By Schirrmacher, Thomas
Copyright©2015 Verlag für Kultur und Wissenschaft
ISBN 13: 978-1-5326-5577-7
Publication date 4/17/2018
Previously published by Verlag für Kultur und Wissenschaft, 2015

Contents

Biographies

David L. Baker

David L. Baker holds a PhD from Sheffield University, England, and has lectured in Old Testament at HKBP Theological Seminary in Pematang Siantar, North Sumatra, Indonesia; Jakarta Theological Seminary, Indonesia; and Trinity Theological College, Perth, Australia. He has also served as deputy warden of Tyndale House, Cambridge. He is the author of several books and many articles, in English and Indonesian. Recent works include *Tight Fists or Open Hands? Wealth and Poverty in Old Testament Law* (Eerdmans), and contributions to *The God of Covenant* (Apollos), *Transforming the World* (Inter-Varsity), and *As Long as the Earth Endures* (Apollos). At present he lives in Cambridge, England, continuing to teach and write, with particular interests in the Decalogue, biblical theology, and economic and environmental ethics.

John Warwick Montgomery

John Warwick Montgomery is Distinguished Research Professor of Philosophy, Concordia University Wisconsin (USA), and Professor Emeritus of Law and Humanities at the University of Bedfordshire (U.K.). His many earned degrees include a Ph.D. (Chicago), D.Théol. (Strasbourg, France), and LL.D. (Cardiff, Wales, U.K.). He is a member of the California, District of Columbia, Virginia, and Washington State bars, as well as the U.S. Supreme Court bar. In addition, he is a Barrister-at-Law in England and Wales and an Avocat à la Cour in Paris and practises at the European Court of Human Rights in Strasbourg. He received the Patriarch's Medal of the Romanian Orthodox Church for his success in the case of Bessarabian Orthodox Church v Moldova before the European Court of Human Rights. Professor Montgomery is the author or editor of more than sixty books in English, French, German, Spanish, and Romanian, and more than a hundred scholarly articles.
Websites: www.jwm.christendom.co.uk, www.apologeticsacademy.eu, and www.newreformationpress.com

Thomas Schirrmacher

Prof. Dr. theol. Dr. phil. Thomas Schirrmacher, PhD, ThD, DD, earned his doctorates in ecumenical theology, in cultural anthropology, and in the sociology of religion. He is professor of social ethics as well as president of Martin Bucer European Theological Seminary and Research Institutes with branches in Bonn, Berlin, Zurich, Innsbruck, Prague, Istanbul and São Paolo, Distinguished Professor of Global Ethics and International Development at William Carey University in Shillong (Meghalaya, India), visiting professor of the sociology of religion at the state University of the West in Timisoara (Romania) and director of the International Institute for Religious Freedom (Bonn, Cape Town, Colombo). As President of the International Council of the International Society for Human Rights and as Ambassador for Human Rights of World Evangelical Alliance (representing Protestant churches with altogether 600 million members), he regularly testifies in parliaments and supreme courts in Europe and the Americas.

Foreword

The Moral Structure of the Condemnation of Slavery in Amos

Thomas K. Johnson

Amos quoted God, "For three sins of Gaza, even for four, I will not turn back my wrath. Because she took captive whole communities and sold them to Edom." (Amos 1:6) The readers knew that Edom was where one went to sell slaves. As God's representative, Amos condemned slave trading and human trafficking in antiquity. Amos continued, "This is what the Lord says: 'For three sins of Tyre, even for four, I will not relent. Because she sold whole communities of captives to Edom, disregarding a treaty of brotherhood, I will send fire on the walls of Tyre that will consume her fortresses.'" (Amos 1:9-10) Gaza was not the only city guilty of selling human souls.

These descriptions of slave trading in the Bible and those that follow in this book should shock our hearts; we should feel sick because of what is happening. But we must not turn off our minds if we wish to follow in the footsteps of Amos. We must notice the ethical structure of the critique of slavery in the Bible and in Christian history. This is what I see:

On the one hand, Amos was directly quoting God's special revelation to Amos; while doing so, he also was applying principles found throughout God's special revelation in those parts of the Hebrew Bible (which we call the Old Testament) which had already been written in his day. The global condemnation of slavery coming from the mouth and pen of Amos was deeply rooted in God's *special* revelation, both as that special revelation had been received long in the past and also recently received directly by Amos. On the other hand, when Amos was speaking to the people of Gaza and Tyre, he condemned the abuse of humans on the basis of God's *natural* or *general* revelation of the moral law, not only on the basis of God's specially revealed moral law in the Bible. The particular groups of people to whom Amos was speaking had not yet received the Bible, yet Amos expected them to know something about the difference between good and evil and to know that buying and selling people was wrong.

A classic evangelical commentator on the prophet Amos, Alec Motyer, observes about the nations surrounding Israel addressed in Amos chapter one, "They have one negative common denominator: none of them had ever received any special revelation of God or of his law; He had never sent prophets to them; there was no Moses in their historical past; ... they were without the law written upon tablets of stone, but they were not without the law written on the conscience."[1] It was the presence of God's moral law as it is naturally or generally revealed among the nations that should have enabled them to perceive the wrongness of their actions when they abused the rights of the weak. They were justly condemned for doing what they knew was evil.

Observing the moral complexity of the proclamation of Amos and his successors may help our modern efforts against slavery and human trafficking. To emphasize the point: when Amos addressed the nations surrounding Israel about their gross inhumanity, he directly quoted God in such a manner that his message was deeply rooted in God's special revelation to Israel and to Amos; at the same time, his message should have found traction among the nations that had not received God's special revelation because they had already received (and perhaps partly suppressed) God's general revelation of his moral law. And this moral complexity is what we see in the history of Christian anti-slavery efforts.

To take only one example, William Wilberforce: his personal faith in Jesus, and therefore his reception of God's special revelation in the Bible and in Christ, was the starting point for his leadership in ending the abomination of slave trading; at the same time, the message of Wilberforce (and of the thousands of Christians who shared his moral convictions arising from the Bible) had an effect in the broader societies of their day, because even those citizens and members of governments and parliaments who did not recognize Jesus or the Bible could begin to perceive the wickedness of slavery. As Amos assumed long ago, even people without the Bible should be able to see that selling and abusing people is wrong, though they might need a prophet to remind them of what they should already know and also to bring God's wrath to mind. Wilberforce and friends wanted people to end slavery and to come to faith in Jesus, but either order was acceptable, whether rejecting slavery before (or perhaps even without) coming to Jesus, or coming to Jesus and then rejecting slavery as a result of repentance and faith.

We hope this little book will add strength to the new efforts to address the abominations of slavery and human trafficking. We need to add

---

[1]   Alec Motyer, *The Message of Amos,* in the Bible Speaks Today series edited by John Stott, Alec Motyer, and Derek Tidball (Downers Grove: InterVarsity Press, 1974), pp. 36-37.

heat to our efforts, but that heat needs to be informed by the light of wisdom, the point of a book like this. The long-term efforts needed to once again abolish the slave trade and slavery will need biblical, historical, and moral studies both to motivate and to guide us.

THE HUMANISATION OF SLAVERY IN OLD TESTAMENT LAW[2]

David L. Baker

Abstract: The existence of slavery seems to be taken for granted in the Old Testament, as elsewhere in the ancient Near East, and Christian readers today often wonder why it is not more clearly condemned. This paper discusses several Old Testament laws relating to slavery, especially Exodus 21:20, 26-27; Leviticus 25:39-41; Deuteronomy 5:13-15; 15:12; 23:15-16; 24:7. It is shown that these laws challenge the status quo by humanising the institution, treating slaves as human beings rather than property. If these laws were followed, the result should have been a reduction in the number of people held as slaves, and improved conditions for those remaining.

During the seventeenth and eighteenth centuries, British slave-ships transported tens of thousands of slaves from Africa to America each year. Altogether millions of ordinary Africans were captured, put in chains, and taken away – never to return home. In 1784 Peter Peckard, vice-chancellor of the University of Cambridge, preached a sermon entitled 'Am I not a man and a brother?' which became a motto of the abolitionist movement. He then held an essay competition with the title, 'Who has the right to enslave someone against their will?' The competition was won by Thomas Clarkson, who was later one of a group of twelve Christians who committed themselves to the abolition of this trade in human beings. They persuaded a young politician called William Wilberforce to become their parliamentary spokesman, and for twenty years they wrote pamphlets, organised petitions, and held debates. Eventually the slave trade was made illegal in the British Empire in 1807, just two hundred years ago.

---

[2]   This article was originally published in *Ethics in Brief* 12.4 (2007). For a detailed study of the laws on slavery, in their ancient Near Eastern context, see my 2009 book: *Tight Fists or Open Hands? Wealth and Poverty in Old Testament Law* (Eerdmans): chapters 5 and 6. I have made my own translation from Hebrew of the laws quoted in this article.

It was a wonderful achievement. A noted nineteenth-century historian described it as one of 'the three or four perfectly virtuous pages in the history of nations' (Lecky). However, an issue arises concerning the role of the Bible in this achievement. On the one hand, opponents of Clarkson and Wilberforce argued that both Old and New Testaments approve of slavery, or at least assume its existence without criticism. On the other hand, the abolitionists believed that their campaign was based on biblical principles. The present paper is concerned to examine this issue in relation to the Old Testament, especially its laws. Does Old Testament law support the continuance of slavery, or its abolition?

At first sight, it is not difficult to make a case for the former view. As elsewhere in the ancient Near East, the existence of slavery seems to be taken for granted in Israel (Gen. 15:3; 16:1; Judg. 6:27; 2 Sam. 9:10) and it is never condemned categorically as an institution. War captives are routinely enslaved (Gen. 34:29; Num. 31:9; Deut. 20:10-11). Existing slaves are bought and sold, and their children become slaves too (Gen. 17:12, 13, 23, 27; Exod. 12:44; Lev. 22:11; 25:44-46).

Nevertheless, the predominant attitude towards slavery in Old Testament law is negative. One of the primary motivations for obedience in the laws on care for the poor and oppressed is the exodus, God's liberation of his people from slavery in Egypt (Lev. 19:34, 36; 25:38, 42; Deut. 5:15; 15:15; 24:18). Unlike neighbouring countries, Israel had no social stratification, and all Israelites were considered brothers and sisters (cf. Lev. 25:39-43; Deut. 15:7-11; 17:15, 20). The Hebrew word translated 'slave' means literally a 'worker', whereas the Akkadian equivalent means 'one who has come down' in social position. Slavery did not fit well with the ideals of Israelite society, and laws were designed to reduce the number of people in slavery and protect slaves who were not actually freed.[3]

---

[3]   Only one law permits chattel slavery (Lev. 25:44-46a), and even this does not encourage it, but limits it to those outside the covenant *community*: residents of other countries and foreign residents in Israel. The law permits buying slaves, not kidnapping; so it concerns acquisition of those who are already slaves, or are offered by sale by their families, not forcible enslaving of free people. In fact, it is part of a longer law, the main point of which is to prohibit slavery for Israelites (vv. 39, 42-43, 46b).

Provision for Holidays

Among all the ancient Near Eastern laws known to us, only those of Israel give workers the right to free time for worship and recreation. For example:

> Six days you shall labour, and do all your work. But the seventh day is a sabbath to the LORD your God; you shall not do any work, you or your son or your daughter, or your male or female slave, or your ox or your donkey or any of your livestock, or your resident alien who is in your town, so that your male or female slave may rest as you do. Remember that you were a slave in the land of Egypt, and the Lord your God brought you out from there. (Deut. 5:13-15; cf. Exod. 20:9-11)

It is striking that the sabbath is to be observed by the whole community, including slaves. The expression 'as you do' is significant in granting equal rights to all human beings with respect to this weekly holiday. If this point had not been emphasised, it is very likely that slaves would have been expected to continue their work while more privileged members of society enjoyed their holy days. The same point is made clear in regulations for observing festivals (Deut. 12:12, 18; 16:11, 14).

Protection from Abuse

There are two laws about slave abuse. The first concerns beating, and its essence is as follows:

> When a man beats his male or female slave with a stick, and the slave dies from the beating, he shall certainly be avenged. (Exod. 21:20)[4]

Beating with a stick or rod was a common method of discipline, especially for children (Prov. 10:13; 13:24; 22:15; 23:13-14). The law assumes slaves will be disciplined in this way, while insisting that masters are sensitive to the physical condition of their slaves and administer punishment accordingly. If they misjudge the situation and a slave dies, they are to be punished. The term 'avenged' probably implies the death penalty, which means that a master who kills his slave is treated as a murderer and receives the same punishment as for killing a free person. Thus the law provides some protection for slaves from cruel treatment by their mas-

---

[4]   The following verse is difficult to interpret and is discussed in detail in my book.

ters, and recognises the life of a slave to be of equal value to that of any other human being.

A second law deals with the case of a slave who suffers permanent bodily injury at the hands of his or her master:

> When a man strikes the eye of his male or female slave and destroys it, he shall let the slave go free [as compensation] for the eye. And if he knocks out the tooth of his male or female slave, he shall let the slave go free [as compensation] for the tooth. (Exod. 21:26-27)

This ruling compares very favourably with the Babylonian Laws of Hammurabi (§199), where masters are compensated for injury to their slaves by third parties but nothing is said about compensation for the slaves themselves. In Israel the master himself is punished for abuse of his slave by being made to forfeit a valuable worker. What is more, the slave is to be freed, even for a relatively minor injury like loss of a tooth.

This pair of laws is unique in the ancient Near East because slave abuse is considered in terms of human rights rather than property rights. Elsewhere slaves were treated as chattels, and abuse laws were designed to compensate the master for loss or damage to his property. Old Testament law, however, emphasises that slaves are to be treated as human beings and ownership of slaves does not permit a master to kill or injure them.

Asylum for Fugitives

A major problem faced by slave-owners was how to stop slaves running away. To make this as difficult as possible, slaves in the ancient Near East were often restrained with fetters or shackles. Many were distinguished by a distinctive hairstyle, or a mark which was branded, incised, or tattooed on their flesh. Inevitably some slaves still escaped, and rewards were offered to anyone who returned a runaway slave. The Laws of Hammurabi demanded capital punishment for anyone who enabled a slave to escape or harboured a fugitive.

When we turn to the Bible we find something completely different:

> You shall not give up a slave to his master, who comes to you for protection from his master. Let him stay with you, in your midst, in the place he chooses in one of your towns, wherever suits him best; you shall not oppress him. (Deut. 23:15-16)

Deuteronomy provides one of the most striking contrasts between Old Testament law and other ancient Near Eastern laws by prohibiting what was elsewhere a fundamental obligation (v. 15). Members of the covenant community are not to return fugitive slaves to their masters, but must provide them with hospitality and a safe refuge (v. 16a). What in Babylon is a capital offence, in Jerusalem is to be an opportunity for kindness and generosity. Like other marginal people, fugitive slaves could very easily be oppressed, but this is forbidden to the people of God (v. 16b).

This law is not only unique in the ancient Near East; it deliberately contradicts the common view that it was a serious offence to help a runaway slave. The principle elsewhere was to maintain the status quo, defending the rights of slave owners to keep their property. In contrast, biblical law focuses on the slave as a human being, emphasising compassion for someone in distress. This echoes Old Testament traditions about Israel's escape from slavery in Egypt, which should make them sympathetic to others in a similar position. As God showed his mercy to them, so they must be merciful to others.

Prohibition of Kidnapping

No-one has the right to deprive another member of the covenant community of their freedom:

> When a person is caught kidnapping a brother, one of the people of Israel, and treats him as a slave or sells him, that kidnapper shall die, and [so] you will purge the evil from your midst. (Deut. 24:7; cf. Exod. 21:16)

Old Testament law prohibits kidnapping, the main purpose of which would be to enslave free citizens or sell them as chattel slaves to others. In practice, in the tightly-knit society of ancient Israel, a kidnapper would be unlikely to keep someone in their possession for long, or try to sell them to another Israelite. Probably they would sell them abroad as soon as possible (cf. Gen. 37:25-28), thus also depriving them of the benefits of living in the covenant community. Forcible enslaving of a free person like this is considered such a serious offence that it carries the death penalty.

Voluntary Slavery and Bonded Labour

The prohibition of forcible enslaving does not rule out the possibility of voluntary slavery. Occasionally serious financial difficulty could result in an Israelite becoming a slave, to pay a debt or provide for their family. The law insists that even voluntary slavery is only to be for a limited period:

> When your Hebrew brother or sister is sold [or 'sells him/herself'] to you, and serves you six years, in the seventh year you shall let them go free from you. (Deut. 15:12; cf. Exod. 21:2)

At the end of that period, they are to be provided with capital to enable a successful return to an independent life (vv. 13-15). This may be seen as an attempt to break the cycle of poverty that would otherwise quickly result in the freed person becoming a slave again. Such temporary slaves are also given the option of becoming permanent members of the household at the end of their six years' service, implying that slaves would be looked after so well that they might prefer to continue in that status rather than claim their freedom (vv. 16-17).

Another possibility for paying off debt was bonded labour, also for a limited term. In this connection, it is emphasised that the labourer is not to be treated as a slave:

> When your brother becomes poor beside you and 'sells' himself to you, you shall not make him serve as a slave. He shall be with you as a hired worker or temporary resident; until the year of jubilee he shall serve with you. Then he shall go from you, together with his children; and he shall return to his own clan, and go back to his ancestral property. (Lev. 25:39-41)

The rules for bonded labour imply that they were intended for a family-head who made the agreement together with his whole family, whereas temporary slavery generally applied to individuals.

Limited-term slavery and bonded labour was made realistic by the Old Testament policy of interest-free loans (Exod. 22:25; Lev. 25:35-38). Elsewhere high interest rates would often mean that such arrangements merely covered interest payments and resulted in lifelong bondage for unfortunate debtors.

Conclusion

The Old Testament portrays Israel as a people who experienced famine in their own land, followed by marginalisation and slavery in a foreign country, and eventually liberation. Those whom God had freed were not to be enslaved again, and were to be compassionate to marginal people in their own country. As a result, slavery was discouraged in the covenant community, though never abolished completely.

Elsewhere in the ancient Near East slavery was accepted without question, and slaves were subject to property law, which focused on the rights of slave owners over their property. Against this background, Old Testament law challenged the status quo by humanising the institution. In Israel slaves themselves had rights and were not considered property but human beings. For example, as we have seen, slaves were entitled to holidays and masters were not allowed to abuse their slaves. Fugitive slaves were to be given asylum instead of being returned to their masters. Forcible enslaving was strictly forbidden, and voluntary slavery was limited in term and ended with generous provision for the freed slave. If these laws were followed, the result should have been a reduction in the number of people held as slaves, and improved conditions for those remaining.

At the beginning of the twenty-first century, we have celebrated the bicentenary of the abolition of the slave trade, and yet there are more slaves in the world today than at any other time in history.[5] Perhaps we should not be too quick to criticise the Old Testament for failing to eliminate slavery! It is arguable that Old Testament law was simply being realistic. Rather than outlawing slavery completely, it established principles for care of the poor and needy, emphasising the individual worth of every human being and treating slaves as persons rather than property. If these humanising principles had been practised consistently, slavery might well have disappeared long before Wilberforce.

For Further Reading

Anti-Slavery International web-site: www.antislavery.org

Baker, David L. (2009), *Tight Fists or Open Hands? Wealth and Poverty in Old Testament Law* (Eerdmans).

Bales, Kevin (1999), *Disposable People: New Slavery in the Global Economy* (University of California Press).

---

[5]   Bales (1999) estimates that there were 27 million slaves at the end of the 20th century. ILO (2005) gives a lower figure of 12.3 million, noting that this is a *minimum* estimate. According to UNODC (2006), human trafficking takes place all over the world today, with 127 countries of origin (mainly developing countries), 137 destination countries (mainly in the industrialised world), and 98 transit countries.

Barclay, John M. G. (2007), '"Am I not a Man and a Brother?" The Bible and the British Anti-Slavery Campaign', *Expository Times* 119: 3-14.

Chirichigno, Gregory C. (1993), *Debt-Slavery in Israel and the Ancient Near East* (JSOT Supplement Series, 141).

ILO (2005), *A Global Alliance against Forced Labour* (International Labour Office).

UNODC (2006), *Trafficking in Persons: Global Patterns* (United Nations Office on Drugs and Crime).

SLAVERY, HUMAN DIGNITY AND HUMAN RIGHTS

John Warwick Montgomery

I. The Paradox

When, a quarter century ago, I taught at the International School of Law, Washington, D.C., we lived in Falls Church, Virginia. I could always get a laugh at Commonwealth parties (Virginia must be so designated—never as a mere "State") by observing that I was having great difficulty finding slaves to proofread my book manuscripts. In today's climate of political correctness, such attempts at humour would be regarded as offensive at best, obnoxious at worst.

In the modern world, every one, everywhere condemns slavery. The formal opposition to it is as powerful as is the universal acclaim for human rights (which are lauded both by doctrinaire liberals and by the worst of dictators). Indeed, the international legal instruments could not be more specific—from the Slavery Convention of the League of Nations, which entered into force 9 March 1927, through Article 4 of both the Universal Declaration of Human Rights and the European Convention of Human Rights, to the Supplementary Convention on the Abolition of Slavery, the Slave Trade, and Institutions and Practices Similar to Slavery, adopted in 1956 under UN sponsorship to reinforce and augment the 1927 Slavery Convention. Not only is traditional, chattel slavery declared to be unqualifiedly illegal ("No one shall be held in slavery or servitude; slavery and the slave trade shall be prohibited in all their forms"—Universal Declaration of 1948), but the category of slavery is expanded (1956-1957 Supplementary Convention) to include:

1) Debt bondage, that is to say, the status or condition arising from a pledge by a debtor of his personal services or of those of a person under his control as security for a debt, if the value of those services as reasonably assessed is not applied towards the liquidation of the debt or the length and nature of those services are not respectively limited and defined;

2) Serfdom, that is to say, the condition or status of a tenant who is by law, custom or agreement bound to live and labour on land belonging

to another person and to render some determinate service to such other person, whether for reward or not, and is not free to change his status;

3) Any institution or practice whereby:
   a) A woman, without the right to refuse, is promised or given in mar-
      riage on payment of a consideration in money or in kind to her par-
      ents, guardian, family or any other person or group; or
   b) The husband of a woman, his family, or his clan, has the right to
      transfer her to another person for value received or otherwise; or
   c) A woman on the death of her husband is liable to be inherited by
      another person;
4) Any institution or practice whereby a child or young person under the
   age of 18 years, is delivered by either or both of his natural parents or
   by his guardian to another person, whether for reward or not, with a
   view to the exploitation of the child or young person or of his labour.

The countries ratifying these international treaties cover virtually the
entire globe. Thus—to take but one example—the Supplementary Convention just quoted has been ratified by 119 States-parties, from Afghani-
stan in 1966 (!) to Zimbabwe in 1998 (!!). The *de jure* situation, then, appears entirely unambiguous: slavery, direct or indirect, anywhere and
everywhere, is a legal wrong in every respect, whatever the terminology
applied to it.

Paradoxically, however, things are much different *de facto*. Responsi-
ble anti-slavery organisations cite innumerable instances of the continuing enslavement of human beings by their fellows. The American Anti-
Slavery Group (www.iabolish.com) cites the documented prevalence of
carpet slaves (especially child labourers in the weaving trade) in India[6];
debt slavery in Haiti's sugar industry; sex slaves in Southeast Asia; and
even literal chattel slavery persisting in Mauritania and Sudan. From the
website just given, here is a sobering list of "slavery hotspots":

- THAILAND: Women and children forced to work as sex slaves for tourists
- IVORY COAST: Boys forced to work on cocoa plantations
- INDIA: Children trapped in debt bondage roll beedi cigarettes 14 hours a
  day

---

[6] Cf. Joanna Watson, "Modern Day Slavery," *The Christian Lawyer: The Journal of the
Lawyers' Christian Fellowship* [U.K.], Summer, 2004, pp. 10-11. A useful popular article on the continuing problem of slavery ("21st Century Slaves"), with biblio-
graphical references, may be found in *National Geographic* (September, 2003). For
a scholarly journal devoted to studies in the field of the present paper, see *Slavery & Abolition: A Journal of Slave and Post-Slave Studies* (Routledge).

- SUDAN: Arab militias from the North abduct black African women and children in slave raids
- DOMINICAN REPUBLIC: Haitians lured across the border are forced to cut cane on sugar plantations
- ALBANIA: Teenage girls are tricked into sex slavery and trafficked by organised crime rings
- BRAZIL: Lured into the rainforest, families burn trees into charcoal at gunpoint
- UNITED ARAB EMIRATES: Little Bangladeshi boys are imported to be jockeys for camel racing
- UNITED STATES: 50,000 trafficked in each year, as sex slaves, domestics, seamstresses, and agricultural workers
- BURMA: The ruling military junta exploits civilian forced labour for infrastructure projects
- GHANA: Families repent for sins by giving daughters as slaves to fetish priests
- PAKISTAN: Children with "nimble fingers" are forced to weave carpets in dark looms
- MAURITANIA: Arabo-Berbers buy and sell black Africans as inheritable property

That this catalogue of inhuman activities is by no means exaggerated is illustrated by a 21 February 2004 *Times* (London) news article, "Brazilian Slaves Are Freed in Jungle Raid":

> Forty-nine men, women and children, who had been subjected to months of enforced labour, clearing jungle vegetation from the Fazenda Macauba cattle ranch were freed after telling inspectors that they had spent at least 80 days working 10 hours a day, without pay. . . .
> The raid on the Fazenda Macauba was triggered after [an escapee] reported the conditions to the Pastoral Earth Commission, a Roman Catholic organisation that campaigns against slavery in Brazil. . . .
> The raid . . . is the latest in a recent crackdown on modern slavery, a practice still common in Brazil, especially in the cattle ranches of the Amazon and sugar and coffee plantations in the states of Bahia and Maranhao.
> . . .
> President da Silva has pledged his Government to freeing at least 25,000 people estimated to be in slavery. "A modern Brazil cannot tolerate such an archaic practice," he said.

Slavery, in short, is by no means a dead issue. Such statistics as "the sixty-six slaveholding societies in the Murdock world sample" and the classification of "the large-scale slave systems" presented by sociologist Orlando Patterson, though valuable historically, do not by any means exhaust the subject.[7]

The widespread continuation of slavery practices, paradoxically combined with universal condemnation of the phenomenon, is highlighted by a passage at the end of one of the works of the most distinguished English-language historian of slavery, David Brion Davis of Yale University:

> As Conor Cruise O'Brien has pointed out, the United Nations is political theater dominated by an institutional tone of "lofty morality" perfectly suited for the dramatic exploitation of guilt—in particular, "Western guilt feelings toward the non-white world." The influx of new African states enabled the nonwhite members to win hegemonic control over the "moral conscience of mankind." Unfortunately, condemnations of colonialism and apartheid as the twentieth-century equivalents of slavery sometimes served to shield forms of oppression for which whites bore no responsibility. In a complacent report of 1965, the Republic of Mali contended that a benign, paternalistic servitude had preceded European colonization and that national independence, accompanied by genuine social democracy, had brought the final abolition of slavery and similar institutions. Yet slave-trading continued to flourish in Mauritania, Mali, Niger, and Chad, along the drought-stricken southern fringe of the Sahara. Historical mythology minimizing or denying African and Arab involvement in the slave trade has fostered the false assumption that slavery depended for its survival on colonial regimes.[8]

The source of the paradox of continuing slavery is not "colonialism" or any other related stereotype; its roots lie much deeper, in the conceptions of the human person and in the *Weltanschauungen* which inform those conceptions. In a syllabus for a graduate course in "Slavery As a Critique of the Concept of Human Rights," Professor Raymond Fleming of Florida State University's Department of Modern Languages and Linguistics, put it well:

---

[7]   Orlando Patterson, *Slavery and Social Death: A Comparative Study* (Cambridge, Mass.: Harvard University Press, 1982), pp. 345-64.

[8]   David Brion Davis, *Slavery and Human Progress* (New York: Oxford University Press, 1984), pp. 318-19. Cf. Davis, *Challenging the Boundaries of Slavery* (Cambridge, Mass.: Harvard University Press, 2003), and Thomas Bender (ed.), *The Antislavery Debate: Capitalism and Abolitionism As a Problem in Historical Interpretation* (Berkeley, Ca.: University of California Press,1992) [with contributions by David Brion Davis].

Our attention to the various forms of slavery will enable us to focus upon what Western culture wishes to affirm or deny about the notion of a human subject. Whether it is the Scholastics in the Middle Ages affirming man as a *res sacra*, a sacredness, or Pico della Mirandola in the Renaissance asserting the dignity of man, or Thomas Jefferson proclaiming the self-evident character of specific human rights, we will note along this continuum just how society and *Realpolitik* invariably undermine such declarations. We will see how slavery provides us with an effective critique of the rhetoric of "high culture," and also how the existence of slavery in the face of such sentiments reveals what these utterances leave out of their formulations. What are often left out, what Roland Barthes terms, "what goes without saying," are the ideologies informing such declarations.

Though we shall certainly not engage in the deconstruction here suggested, we shall indeed focus upon the "ideologies" which underlie both the attitudes and the declarations relating to slavery. Our purpose will be to discover what kind of foundation, if any, can put paid to the hypocrisy so often met with in treatments of the phenomenon of slavery.

II. Philosophical Opposition to Slavery

The chief modern philosophical arguments against slavery have been those of Enlightenment natural law theory and Kantian and neo-Kantian universalism. These, alone or in combination, have provided the underpinning for most contemporary human rights philosophies and their opposition to all forms of slavery. The question remains, however: Are these theories adequate?

The jusnaturalism of the French *philosophes* and American "founding fathers" such as Jefferson maintained that there is a built-in ethic of human dignity which all must recognise. The human person benefits from "certain inalienable rights," including the rights to "life, liberty, and the pursuit of happiness." Both the French Declaration of the Rights of Man and the American Bill of Rights endeavoured to summarise the essential civil liberties of the citizen. These rights were supposed to be justified by the agreement of all rational persons. After all, did not the 18th century Enlightenment usher in an "Age of Reason" (Thomas Paine's profoundly influential book title), elevating mankind beyond prior centuries of theological superstition?

Unhappily, this humanistic version of jusnaturalism was—and is— incapable of providing the needed bulwark against slavery. In classical Roman jurisprudence, to which the Enlightenment advocates of the viewpoint frequently turned for their main historical precedent, slavery was allowed by way of the *Ius gentium* ("law of nations/international law") even though it was directly contrary to the natural law: "Slavery is the only case in which, in the extant sources of Roman law, a conflict is declared to exist between the *Ius Gentium* and the *Ius Naturale*. It is of course inconsistent with that universal equality of man which Roman speculations on the Law of Nature assume."[9]

The same ambivalence was present in the thinking versus the practice of French and American Enlightenment revolutionaries. The Marquis de Condorcet, biographer of Voltaire and committed anti-Christian progressive, ruefully admitted that "only a few *philosophes* have from time to time dared raise a cry in favour of humanity [over against slaveholding]."[10] Thomas Jefferson's views of equality did not preserve him from anti-Semitism[11]—much less from a quietist maintenance of the status quo where slaveholding was concerned. It appears likely that he fathered illegitimate children whose mother was one of his slaves.[12] Even a Jefferson hagiographer has to write:

> Jefferson's perception of slavery was determined by several ambivalent circumstances: he was a planter-slaveowner, a Virginian whose strongest allegiance, when the test came, was to his state and section, and withal a man of the eighteenth century Enlightenment. This circumstance created in Jefferson's mind an ambiguity and a dissonance which he never succeeded in resolving to his own satisfaction. While Jefferson regarded slavery as a "hideous evil," the bane of American society, and wholly irreconcilable with his ideal of "republican virtue," he was never able wholly to cast aside the prejudices and the fears which he had absorbed from his surroundings toward people of color; he did not free himself from dependence upon slave labor; and, in the end, he made the expansion of slavery into

---

9   W. W. Buckland, *The Roman Law of Slavery: The Condition of the Slave in Private Law from Augustus to Justinian* (reprint ed.;Cambridge, England: Cambridge University Press, 1970), p. 1.

10 M. J. A. Condorcet, *Remarques sur les Pensées de Pascal*, in Condorcet's *Oeuvres* (12 vols.; Paris: Firmin-Didot, 1847-1849), III, 649.

11 Cf. Arthur Hertzberg, *The French Enlightenment and the Jews* (New York: Columbia University Press, 1990).

12 Cf. Lucia Stanton, *Slavery at Monticello* (Monticello, Virginia: Thomas Jefferson Memorial Foundation, 1996), pp. 20-22, 50 (note 21 and the literature there cited). In his Preface to this monograph, Julian Bond writes that the "gross imbalance he [Jefferson] represents between national promise and execution remains our greatest state embarrassment today."

the territories a constitutional right, and a *conditio sine qua non* of the South's adherence to the Union.[13]

I have pointed elsewhere to law professor and distinguished Federal judge John T. Noonan's demonstration that "Jefferson and his legal mentor George Wythe aided in perpetuating a forensic vocabulary that classed blacks as transferable property, thereby permitting whites to carry on slavery while 'democratically' supporting human freedom and dignity in the founding documents of the nation."[14]

Why did these Enlightenment thinkers suffer from such a disparity between their principles and their practice? As with the Roman jurisprudents, the reason lies surely in the vagueness and ambiguity of their "natural law" principles.[15] Nowhere is the content of the natural law set forth with sufficient explicitness to counter the indignities suffered by those in slavery. Thus rationalisation could easily enter the picture when concrete questions were raised as to the ethical treatment of slaves and the proper criteria of manumission.

Eighteenth-century secular jusnaturalism was later to suffer a devastating blow when in the 19th and 20th centuries anthropologists demonstrated the wide diversity of cultural patterns in non-Western societies. Apparently, not everyone agreed with the "rationality" of enlightened Europeans. Slavery was practised and condoned in many cultures; was it therefore really contrary to the "natural law"? And suppose everyone *had* been against it—would general agreement (*consensus gentium*) suddenly have become a satisfactory test of truth?

As for the ethical theories deriving from Immanuel Kant's Categorical Imperative ("act only on that maxim which you can will to be a universal law"), they have fared no better as a bulwark against slavery. When neo-Kantian John Rawls tells us that we should act under a "veil of ignorance" as to our special advantages and therefore follow utilitarian "principles of justice," treating our fellowmen as equal in rights and dignity, the historical response has generally been that our special advantages are precisely our ground for *not* treating others (such as potential or actual

---

[13]   John Chester Miller, *The Wolf by the Ears: Thomas Jefferson and Slavery* (New York: Free Press, 1977), pp. 2-3. Cf. Matthew T. Mellon, *Early American Views on Negro Slavery* (Boston: Meador, 1934), especially pp. 120-22.

[14]   John Warwick Montgomery, *The Shaping of America* (revised ed.; Minneapolis: Bethany, 1981), p. 54. See Noonan's *Persons and Masks of the Law* (New York: Farrar, Straus & Giroux, 1975).

[15]   John Warwick Montgomery, *The Law Above the Law* (Minneapolis: Bethany, 1975), especially pp. 37-42.

slaves) as we would want to be treated. When Alan Gewirth insists that you rationally "act in accord with the generic rights of your recipients as well as of yourself," not because you are someone special ("Wordsworth Donisthorpe"), the slaver will invariably respond that it is precisely because he *is* "Wordsworth Donisthorpe"—or someone else of superior power, influence, or connections—that he is in a position to function as slavetrader or slaveowner. The Genghis Khans of this world have seldom been impressed by arguments of rationalistic universalisation.[16]

Kantian and neo-Kantian arguments suffer from the same difficulty as claims made on the basis of humanistic jusnaturalism: they do not define adequately the content of ethical action; they do not specify *which* specific actions and activities are good and *which* are bad. Recently, the international press has had a field day with the trial of one Armin Meiwes, who advertised on the net (his occupation was computer programmer) for those who would like him to eat them. After having consumed a number of willing victims, Mr Meiwes was arrested on the charge of having murdered at least one of them. However, he was not convicted of murder but was sentenced by a Kassel court to a mere eight-and-a-half year prison term on the ground that—to quote the judge—"this was an act between two ... people who both wanted something from each other."[17] Suppose that we grant that the eator would have been willing to become the eatee, or vice-versa; would such universalisation of cannibalism therefore establish the ethics of anthropophagy? Surely not; but this means that one must be able to set forth and justify solidly grounded ethical strictures against cannibalism—and slavery—in order to oppose those practices. Merely stating a formal principle of "generic consistency" will hardly be adequate.

Moreover, even supposing that one could successfully demonstrate the correctness of a natural-law ethic or categorical imperative, would this mean that people would necessarily follow it? Must one be rational, when rationality goes against self-interest? History certainly does not support the view that just because one can show that a course of action is right, people will take that route. Quite clearly, to deal with the issue of slavery, one must *change the slavetrader's or slaveowner's value-system.* His

---

[16] On the neo-Kantian attempts to establish a foundation for ethics, see our detailed critiques in John Warwick Montgomery, *Human Rights and Human Dignity* (rev. ed.; Edmonton, Alberta, Canada: Canadian Institute for Law, Theology and Public Policy, 1995), especially pp. 92-98, 183; and *Tractatus Logico-Theologicus* (rev. ed.; Bonn, Germany: Verlag für Kultur und Wissenschaft, 2003), 5.5 – 5.6 (pp. 171-74).

[17] *Washington Times,* 31 January 2004 (UPI dispatch).

or her motivations must undergo radical alteration. In traditional terminology, what is required is *conversion*. But this is precisely what—in spite
of all the good will exercised—humanistic ethics has never been able to
produce. Doubtless this is why the abolition of slavery, insofar as it has
been accomplished, stemmed not from Roman law, naturalistic ethics, or
the Enlightenment, but from the impact of Christian faith.

III. Slavery and Christian Witness

Christianity—Orthodox, Catholic, and Protestant—has always maintained
that (1) God has spoken revelationally, providing absolute standards for
human conduct, and (2) through a personal relationship with Jesus
Christ, the Son of God, who died on the Cross to expiate human sin and
selfishness, one can be transformed ethically, receiving a "new spirit"
and a new value-system which will result in treating the neighbour as
oneself. In principle, therefore, the revealed Christian gospel has the
needed answer to the slavery problem. Has this been the case in practice?

Jewish scholar E. E. Urbach asserts that neither "in classical Greek literature, in the writings of the Stoics, and in the Christian Scriptures . . .
nor in the Jewish sources is there the slightest suggestion of any notions
of the abolition of slavery."[18] We would agree as to all of the above—save
"the Christian Scriptures." To be sure, no call to social revolution occurs
there (and the immediate elimination of slavery in the Roman world
would have produced just that). But the central teaching of Jesus to
"treating the neighbour as oneself," coupled with the changed hearts of
those who came to believe in him, meant the eventual death of a system
based on treating the slave as a chattel and not as a human being worth
as much as his master.

> In such an economic context [that of the Roman Empire] it was virtually
> impossible for anyone to conceive of abolishing slavery as a legal-economic
> institution. To have turned all the slaves into free day laborers would have
> been to create an economy in which those at the bottom would have suf-
> fered even more insecurity and potential poverty than before. To be sure,
> according to all known traditions, neither Jesus nor His immediate follow-
> ers owned slaves; nor did Paul, Barnabas, or Timothy. So both the example
> of Jesus and His great concern for the poor proved to be a challenge for
> many early Christians to conceive of themselves as living already among
> themselves in an alternative social-legal environment (note how Paul ap-

---

[18]   E. E. Urbach, *The Laws Regarding Slavery: As a Source for Social History of the Period of
the Second Temple, the Mishnah and Talmud* (New York: Arno Press, 1979), pp. 93-94.

peals to Philemon to release Onesimus sooner than he may have planned). For the author of 1 Clem. 55:2 Christ's love working through humble spirits has motivated some Christians to sell themselves in order to have money to buy the freedom of others (see Shep. Henn. Mand. 8:10; Sim. 1:8; Ign. Polyc.4:3).[19]

* * * * *

Le maître devait ménager les esclaves comme ses égaux en liberté; il devait les ménager encore comme étant lui-même leur frère en servitude; c'est une autre face de la verité chrétienne que les Pères développent à l'envi, pour mieux faire entrer dans les âmes le sentiment des devoirs de l'egalité. Nous sommes tous nés en servitude, nous sommes tous rachetés en Jesus-Christ. . . .

Ainsi, du moment où le christianisme eut révélé sa doctrine, la cause de la liberté avait vaincu. Le jour du triomphe devait se faire attendre, il est vrai; et déjà le signe du salut dominait dans le monde, qu'on l'attendait encore. Mais pendant ces retards forcés l'Eglise n'oublia point les esclaves; et, en même temps qu'elle leur préparait des ressources désormais honorables après l'affranchissement, elle prétendait leur faire donner une place au foyer domestique, dans l'éducation de la famille, dans l'estime publique; elle réclamait pour eux tous les droits et les traitements de l'homme libre, sauf le droit de disposer de soi, que l'homme libre d'ailleurs cessa bientôt presque généralement d'avoir lui-même.[20]

---

[19] S. Scott Bartchy, "Slavery," *International Standard Bible Encyclopedia*, ed. Geoffrey W. Bromiley (rev. ed., 4 vols.; Grand Rapids, Mich.: Eerdmans, 1979-1988), IV, 546. See also Markus Barth and Helmut Blanke, "The Social Background: Slavery at Paul's Time," in their *The Letter to Philemon: A New Translation with Notes and Commentary* (Grand Rapids, Mich.: Eerdmans, 2000), pp. 1-102.

[20] Henri Wallon, *Histoire de l'esclavage dans l'Antiquité*, ed. Jean Christian Dumont (Paris: Robert Laffont, 1988), pp. 801, 835. This magisterial 19th century work remains of immense importance on the subject of slavery in the ancient world and the Christian impact upon it. On the reference in the first quoted paragraph to redemption from slavery in Jesus Christ, see an important study of the New Testament use of slavery motifs to characterise every human being's bondage to sin and the primary need to be freed from it: Dale B. Martin, *Slavery As Salvation: The Metaphor of Slavery in Pauline Christianity* (New Haven, Conn.: Yale University Press, 1990). In the second quoted paragraph, Wallon's reference in the final two lines is to the soon-to-come barbarian invasions of the Roman Empire and the establishment of feudal serfdom as a desperate attempt at economic stability in the decentralised chaos of the early Middle Ages.

It is an unarguable historical fact that the abolition of slavery in modern times stems directly from Christian influence.[21] We shall briefly review the pertinent ideological background, with special reference to the Anglo-American struggle against slavery and its worldwide repercussions.

The stage was set for the British outlawing of the slave trade and American abolition by Christian theologians, pamphleteers, and preachers from Reformation times to the 19th century. The distinguished German Lutheran theologian J. F. Buddeus (1667-1729), author, *inter alia,* of *Selecta juris naturae et gentium,* argued that even if some blacks were legally captured or received criminal convictions leading to slavery, their offspring should not be subject to bondage by inheritance.[22]

Quakers were especially strong in condemning slavery per se. Benjamin Lay declared in 1736: "*As God gave his only begotten Son, that whosoever believed in him might have everlasting Life; so the Devil gives his only begotten Child, the Merchandize of Slaves and Souls of Men, that whosoever believes and trades in it might have everlasting Damnation.*"[23] Quaker John Woolman, in his *Journal* and his *Some Considerations on the Keeping of Negroes,* devastatingly set forth as a Christian argument the selfishness, immorality and greed inherent in the slave trade and prophetically predicted dire consequences for the future of America if slavery was not eliminated.[24]

In England, Bishop Warburton likewise condemned slavery in the American colonies. Before the Society for the Propagation of the Gospel he declared: "Gracious God! To talk (as in herds of Cattle) of Property in rational Creatures!"[25] Christian apologist William Paley characterised slavery as an "abominable tyranny" and "an institution replete with hu-

---

[21]   Alvin J. Schmidt, *Under the Influence: How Christianity Transformed Civilization* (Grand Rapids, Mich.: Zondervan, 2001), chap. 11 ("Slavery Abolished: A Christian Achievement"), pp. 272-91.

[22]   See the biographical article in the *Allgemeine Deutsche Biographie.*

[23]   Benjamin Lay, *All Slave-keepers that Keep the Innocent in Bondage ...* (Philadelphia, 1737), p. 10-13.

[24]   David Brion Davis concludes his magisterial study, *The Problem of Slavery in Western Culture* (Ithaca, N.Y.: Cornell University Press, 1966), with "Epilogue: John Woolman's Prophecy" (pp. 483-93).

[25]   William Warburton, *A Sermon Preached Before the Incorporated Society for the Propagation of the Gospel in Foreign Parts* (London, 1766), pp. 25-26. The Warburton Lectures, devoted by the terms of Warburton's bequest to the defence of the Christian faith, continue today at Lincoln's Inn (one of the four barristers' Inns of Court), London.

man misery" which could no longer possibly be justified, even on utilitarian grounds.[26]

John Wesley, the Anglican founder of Methodism, asserted that "the dreadful consequence of slavery is the same amongst every people and in every nation where it prevails." To the slaveowner he declared: "Thy hands, thy bed, thy furniture, thy house, thy lands are at present stained with blood" as a result of using slave labour, and only repentance before God and emancipation could put things right.[27]

John Newton's dramatic conversion from slave trader to clergyman had tremendous impact in changing the English climate of opinion. It was Newton who not only composed such classic hymns as "Amazing Grace," "How Sweet the Name of Jesus Sounds," and "Glorious Things of Thee Are Spoken,"[28] but who also spoke uncompromisingly against the unchristian activity with which he had formerly been connected.[29] Newton's autobiography was circulating in a cheap, popular edition in France in the years immediately prior to the abolition of slavery in the French colonies (1848).[30] Wesley and Newton are excellent illustrations of what David Brion Davis has termed the "important connection between evangelical religion and antislavery."[31]

---

[26] William Paley, *The Principles of Moral and Politcal Philosophy* (London, 1785), pp. 196-98 (cf. "Introduction").

[27] John Wesley, *Thoughts upon Slavery* (Philadelphia, 1774), especially pp. 39-55.

[28] On Newton's hymnody, see my former professor Erik Routley's *I'll Praise My Maker: Studies in English Classical Hymnody* (London: Independent Press, 1951), pp. 145-78. The most accessible primary source on Newton's life is the contemporary biography by Richard Cecil; it has been responsibly edited and updated by Marylynn Rousse: *The Life of John Newton* (Geanies House,Fearn, Ross-shire, Great Britain: Christian Focus Publications, 2000). The Cowper and Newton Museum in Olney, Bucks, is well worth visiting; Newton was pastor in Olney "near sixteen years" (Newton's epitaph).

[29] John Newton, *Thoughts Upon the African Slave Trade* (2d ed.; London, 1788); Newton's *Journal of a Slave Trader* (1750-54) and *Thoughts Upon the African Slave Trade* were reprinted in one volume by Epworth Press in 1962. Cf. Gail Cameron and Stan Crooke, *Liverpool—Capital of the Slave Trade* (Liverpool, England: Picton Press, 1992), and James Walvin, *Black Ivory: Slavery in the British Empire* (2d ed.; Oxford: Blackwell, 2001).

[30] *Récit authentique de la Vie de J. Newton ... écrit par lui-même dans une suite de lettres adressées au Docteur Haweis* [Toulouse: J.-M. Corne, 1835]). Copy in the author's personal library.

[31] Davis, *The Problem of Slavery in Western Culture (op. cit.)*, p. 388-90. See also D. Bruce Hindmarsh, *John Newton and the English Evangelical Tradition* (Grand Rapids, Mich.; Eerdmans, 2001), and Adam Hochschild, *Bury the Chains: Prophets and Rebels in the Fight to Free an Empire's Slaves* (New York: Houghton Mifflin, 2005).

These believers from a wide variety of confessional traditions provided the backdrop for the political action that finally succeeded in destroying slavery in England and America.[32] The chief names associated with that activity in England were Granville Sharp and William Wilberforce. Both of them were directly and centrally motivated by their Christian convictions.

Granville Sharp (1735-1813) is still a household name in New Testament scholarship, for he formulated the rule bearing his name which recognises that "when two personal nouns of the same case and connected by the copulate *kai,* if the former has the definite article and the latter has not, they both belong to the same person." This rule is of tremendous theological importance, for it establishes, in passages such as 2 Thessalonians 1:12, the identity of Jesus Christ with God the Father.[33] Sharp was one of the founders of the British and Foreign Bible Society and of the Society for the Conversion of the Jews.

But Granville Sharp's undying fame rests on his success in abolishing the slave trade. As the inscription on his monument in Poets' Corner, Westminster Abbey has it:

> He took his post among the foremost of the honourable band
> Associated to deliver Africa from the rapacity of Europe,
> By the abolition of the Slave Trade.
> Nor was death permitted to interrupt his career of usefulness,
> Till he had witnessed that Act of the British Parliament
> By which the abolition was decreed.

In 1767, Sharp encountered a West Indian planter's slave named Jonathan Strong who had been brought to London and badly beaten by his master;

---

[32] Cf. Thomas Clarkson, *The History of the Rise, Progress, and Accomplishment of the Abolition of the African Slave-trade by the British Parliament* (2 vols., reprint ed.; London: Frank Cass, 1968), especially I, 5-192 and II, 570-87. This classic work by one who devoted his life to opposing slavery internationally was originally published in 1808, immediately following the British Parliament's outlawing of the slave trade. Clarkson declares (I, 8-9): "Among the evils, corrected or subdued, either by the general influence of Christianity on the minds of men, or by particular associations of Christians, the African Slave-trade appears to me to have occupied the foremost place." Cf. Melvin D. Kennedy, *Lafayette and Slavery: From His Letters to Thomas Clarkson and Granville Sharp* (Easton, Pa.: American Friends of Lafayette, 1950).

[33] Granville Sharp, *Remarks on the Uses of the Definitive Article in the Greek Text of the New Testament, Containing many New Proofs of the Divinity of Christ . . .,* ed. William David McBrayer (reprint ed.; Atlanta/Roswell, Ga.: Original Word, 1995).

once recovered, he was sold by the master to a third party. Sharp was so incensed by this that he examined the legal situation for himself and finally, five years later, in the *Somersett* case, succeeded in obtaining Lord Mansfield's judgment: "The state of slavery is so odious that nothing can be suffered to support it but positive law, and there is no law."[34] This meant, in effect, that a slave must forthwith receive freedom the moment he or she set foot on English soil.[35]

The forty-year-long, ultimately successful struggle of William Wilberforce (1759-1833) to obtain a Parliamentary act abolishing slavery is too well known to require detailed discussion here; the literature is extensive.[36] What needs to be stressed is Wilberforce's root motivation in engaging in this formidable task: his Christian conviction that slavery was an offense to almighty God and a detriment to the effective spread of Christ's gospel.[37] Wilberforce experienced evangelical conversion in his 20's and came under the influence of former slave trader John Newton. In 1787, he declared: "God has set before me two great objects: the abolition of the slave trade and the reformation of manners." From that point he never looked back. As one of the leaders of the so-called "Clapham Sect"—evangelicals who promoted political, philanthropic, and ethical causes—he championed prison reform, Bible distribution, missionary endeavour, and charitable work of many kinds. In his crusade against slav-

---

[34] Cf. Steven M. Wise, *Though the Heavens May Fall: The Landmark Trial That Led to the End of Human Slavery* (Boston: Merloyd Lawrence, 2005).

[35] See Granville Sharp, *A Tract on the Law of Nature, and Principles of Action in Man* (London: B. White; and E. and C. Dilly, 1777), and *Tracts on Slavery and Liberty: The Just Limitation of Slavery in the Laws of God . . . The Law of Passive Obedience . . . The Law of Liberty . . .* (reprint ed.; Westport, Conn.: Negro Universities Press, 1969). Cf. Edward C. P. Lascelles, *Granville Sharp and the Freedom of Slaves in England* (London: Oxford University Press/Humphrey Milford, 1928) [with extensive documentation and illustrations]; Oliver Ransford, *The Slave Trade: The Story of Transatlantic Slavery* (Newton Arrot, Devon, England: Readers Union, 1972), pp. 178 ff.; and Daniel B. Wallace, "Granville Sharp: A Model of Evangelical Scholarship and Social Activism," *Journal of the Evangelical Theological Society*, XLI/4 (December 1998), 591-613.

[36] Leonard W. Cowie, *William Wilberforce, 1759-1833: A Bibliography* (Westport, Conn.: Greenwood, 1992).

[37] See especially: John Pollock, *Wilberforce* (London: Constable, 1977); David J. Vaughan and George Grant, *Statesman and Saint: The Principled Politics of William Wilberforce* (Nashville, Tenn.: Cumberland House, 2001); Kevin Belmonte, *Hero for Humanity: A Biography of William Wilberforce* (Colorado Springs, Colo.: NavPress, 2002)—and, to be sure, Leslie Stephen's classic article on him in the *Dictionary of National Biography*.

ery as a Member of Parliament, he first succeeded after eighteen years in seeing the slave trade outlawed (1807-1808), and then, after another twenty-six years, the passing of the Emancipation Bill (in 1833, just three days before his demise).

The efforts of Wilberforce and likeminded English opponents of slavery had an impact far beyond Great Britain. Their "transcendent belief stirred abolitionists in the United States during the antebellum and Civil War periods, in France during the 1840s, in Cuba during the Ten Years' War (1868-78), and in Brazil during the 1880s."[38]

In America, the English evangelical impact is clear, for example, in the writings of Thomas Branagan of Philadelphia (1774-1843), like Newton personally involved in slaving and subsequently converted to Christian belief.[39] In his essay on "Human Slavery," he refers specifically to Wilberforce's Parliamentary struggles and declares: "Slavery, hateful to God and man, and the greatest evil and sum-total of all evils under the sun, and inflicted by Americans, the most favoured people, and, may I not say, the most enlightened and highest in profession of liberty and Christianity, must render us the most inexcusable, and draw down, unless expiated by sincere repentance and undoing heavy burdens, the just indignation of Him who does not even let a sparrow fall without his notice."[40]

The American abolition movement drew its power directly from Christian sources. Harriet Beecher Stowe, the author *Uncle Tom's Cabin* (1851-52), the most influential anti-slavery fiction ever written, selling on publication a half a million copies in the United States and double that number in Great Britain, was the daughter of the Revd Lyman Beecher, president of Lane Theological Seminary; wife of a Lane Seminary professor; and sister of the celebrated preacher Henry Ward Beecher. She began writing her novel following a church service in which she had a mystical experience; afterwards she said that "The Lord himself wrote," i.e., was the real author, of her book.[41]

The impact of the Lane Theological Seminary on the abolition movement was considerable.

---

[38] Davis, *Slavery and Human Progress (op. cit.)*, pp. 280-81.

[39] On Branagan, see Lewis Leary, "Thomas Branagan," in his *Soundings: Some Early American Writers* (Athens, Ga.: University of Georgia Press, 1975), pp. 229-52; and Leary, "Thomas Branagan," in James A. Levernier and Douglas R. Wilmes (eds.), *American Writers Before 1800: A Biographical and Critical Dictionary* (Westport, Conn.: Greenwood Press, 1983), pp. 195-96.

[40] [Thomas Branagan,] *The Guardian Genius . . . or, Patriotic Admonitions . . . in relation to . . . Human Slavery. . . . By a Philanthropist* (New York, 1839), pp. 25 ff.

[41] Ransford, *op. cit.*, pp. 235-43.

In 1833 Oberlin College was founded in northern Ohio. Into some of the first classes there women were admitted on equal terms with men. In 1835 the trustees offered the presidency to Professor Asa Mahan, of Lane Seminary. He was himself an abolitionist from a slave State, and he refused to be President of Oberlin College unless negroes were admitted on equal terms with other students. Oberlin thus became the first institution in the country which extended the privileges of the higher education to both sexes of all races. It was a distinctly religious institution devoted to radical reforms of many kinds.[42] Oberlin College

Far less well known than Harriet Beecher Stowe were an influential number of Christian writers who condemned American slavery. As early as 1816, George Bourne posed the rhetorical question, "Can you conscientiously believe, that a slaveholder exhibits that assimilation to the meek and lowly Jesus, which is indispensable to an enjoyment of the inheritance of the Saints in light?"[43] Slavery was also to be condemned, argued Bourne, because it undermined the God-given institution of marriage.[44]

Charles Elliott (1792-1869), Methodist missionary to the Indians, abolitionist and sometime president of Iowa Wesleyan University, maintained that (1) slaves could not help but hate their oppressors and therefore slavery promoted hateful and murderous thoughts—directly contrary to Jesus' teachings (e.g., Matthew 5:21-22)[45]; (2) slaveholders break up families and necessarily maltreat little children—one of the most heinous of sins according to Jesus (Matthew 18:2-6; cf. Revelation 18:21)[46]; (3) slavery

Good arguments

---

[42]   Jesse Macy, *The Anti-Slavery Crusade: A Chronicle of the Gathering Storm* (New Haven, Conn.: Yale University Press, 1920), pp. 50-51. Fascinatingly, the radical anti-slavery activism of many Lane theological students was more than even that institution could tolerate; a considerable number of students (the so-called "Lane Rebels") decamped to Oberlin in 1834; see Stuart C. Henry, "Lane Theological Seminary," in *Dictionary of Heresy Trials in American Christianity,* ed. George H. Shriver (Westport, Conn.: Greenwood Press, 1997), pp. 214-21.

[43]   George Bourne, *The Book* [i.e., the Bible] *and Slavery Irreconcilable* (Philadelphia: J. M. Sanderson, 1816), p.196.

[44]   Ken Glover, "Jesus on American Slavery: What He Said, What He Did Not Say, and What He Was Said To Have Said," Unpublished Paper Presented at the 55th Annual Meeting of the Evangelical Theological Society, Atlanta, Ga., 20 November 2003.

[45]   Charles Elliott, *Sinfulness of American Slavery: Proved from Its Evil Sources; Its Injustice; Its Wrongs; Its Contrariety to Many Scriptural Commands, Prohibitions, and Principles, and to the Christian Spirit,* ed. B. F. Tefft (2 vols.; Cincinnati, Ohio: Swormstedt & Power, 1850), II, 25. This edition was reprinted by Negro Universities Press in New York in 1968.

[46]   *Ibid.,* I, 87.

keeps the blacks in ignorance, whereas the gospel message requires Christian education (Luke 11:52; John 5:39)[47]; (4) Christ—in Luke 4—effectively incorporated into his teaching and expanded upon the Old Testament special year of Jubilee (when slaves were freed), such that he "established, in his public administrations, a foundation for the universal emancipation of slaves"[48]; and, most important of all, (5) since Jesus redeemed everyone, there can be no justification for one person's enslaving another:

> All men are redeemed by the same blood of Christ; and therefore, this common and general redemption by the blood of Christ is at variance with slavery. . . .
> The same great sacrifice has been made for the slave as for the master; and therefore, the soul of the slave is worth as much as the soul of the master.[49]

The collected volumes of American slave cases also evidence the profound influence of the Christian message on the institution of slavery in the years preceding the American Civil War and emancipation. For example, one Thomas Reynolds of Virginia, a Methodist believer, prepared a testamentary instrument in which he declared that "for certain good causes, but more especially that it is contrary to the command of Christ to keep my fellow creatures in bondage, I do hereby liberate all my slaves." When the slaves in question ultimately sued for their freedom, the lower court refused on the ground that the instrument had not been proved and recorded in a proper court. The case then went to Virginia's Court of Appeals, and its President, the great Henry St. George Tucker (1780-1848) spoke for a unanimous court: "It would be monstrous to say that where a testator retained, till his last breath, the anxious purpose to give effect to a previous deed of emancipation, that purpose should be defeated by his casual death before the session of the probate court." The former slaves were granted their freedom.[50]

---

[47]   *Ibid.,* I, 126.
[48]   *Ibid.,* II, 265-66.
[49]   *Ibid.,* I, 303-305. On Charles Elliott, see the biographical article in the *Dictionary of American Biography*. Another of Elliott's works was entitled, *The Bible and Slavery: in which the Abrahamic and Mosaic Discipline is Considered in Connection with the Most Ancient Forms of Slavery, and the Pauline Code on Slavery as Related to Roman Slavery and the Discipline of the Apostolic Churches* (1857).
[50]   *Manns v. Givens,* 7 Leigh 689 at 718-19 (July 1836): *Judicial Cases concerning American Slavery and the Negro,* ed. Helen T. Catterall (5 vols.; Washington, D. C.: Carnegie Institution, 1926-1937), I, 183-85. Cf. also: Barnett Hollander, *Slavery in America: Its*

The historical and ideological background of such cases is clarified by Philip J. Schwarz:

> Quakers and their associates provided an even better method of escape for some slaves in 1782 when they successfully lobbied in the Old Dominion's legislature for the law that thereafter allowed white emancipators to free any slaves they wanted to by deed without having to petition the state government for a private law. As Quakers, Methodists, and others began to take advantage of this legislation, they created one more ambiguous situation for slaves. The increasing number of individual manumissions for slaves encouraged early abolitionists to put more effort into advocating a general emancipation of the state's slaves.[51]

IV. Concluding Caveats

What do we learn from history for our continuing battle against contemporary forms of slavery? At least four important truths:

First, *we must oppose, root and branch, all forms of modern relativism.* For the post-modern relativist, there are, a priori, no absolutes. Therefore, there is nothing inherently wrong with slavery—though it may be evaluated and perhaps critiqued on (fluctuating) sociological grounds. This will simply not do. Was it not the Third Reich that endeavoured to justify its enslavement (and worse) of Jews by claiming Aryan superiority and therefore sociological, Nietzschean, *Übermensch* exemptions from proper humanitarian standards? Sobering is an argument presented by the eminent Ugaritic scholar Cyrus Gordon:

> ... that it was no crime for men to copulate with animals in Ugarit is indicated by the fact that the favorite god Baal impregnated a heifer (67: V: 17-22), a myth, which, for all we know, may have been enacted ritually by reputable priests. To the Hebrews, on the other hand, copulation with beasts was a heinous crime calling for the death penalty (Ex. 22: l8; Lev. 18: 23; Deut. 27: 21). Moreover, the Bible tells us that the Hebrews' pagan neighbors practised beastiality (Lev. 18: 24), as we now know to be literally true from the Ugaritic documents. All this implies that if we discuss Hebrew criminology, we should include beastiality, for in Hebrew society it

---

Legal History (London: Bowes & Bowes, 1962), and Paul Finkelman, *Slavery in the Courtroom: An Annotated Bibliography of American Cases* (Washington, D. C.: Library of Congress, 1985). On Tucker, see, *inter alia,* the *Biographical Directory of the United States Congress* and the *Dictionary of American Biography.*

[51]   Philip J. Schwarz, *Twice Condemned: Slaves and the Criminal Laws of Virginia, 1705-1865* (Baton Rouge, La.: Louisiana State University Press, 1988), p. 193.

was a crime. However, there is no basis for including beastiality in a treatment of the criminology of Ugarit, since it was not a crime there. ... The test of the significance of a social phenomenon is this: Does the group in question make an issue of it?[52]

This may well serve as an adequate description of social phenomena; it is certainly *not* an adequate way of handling serious ethical issues. If bestiality is wrong, it is wrong under *all* conditions and in *any* society. If slavery is to be condemned, it is to be condemned wherever it occurs. Though tolerated (like divorce) "for the hardness of hearts" under certain past circumstances (Mark 10: 2-9), a moral evil does not become a moral good owing to such concessions. Wrong is wrong, and sociological considerations do not change that fact.

But, secondly, this leads us to the vital point (made earlier) that a transcendent source of ethical principles is the only adequate bulwark against the trivialising of slavery and comparable moral evils. Any other attempted justification of anti-slavery will be no more than human opinion, which, if set forth by humans, can be revoked by humans as the sociological context changes. Thus, we need a religious foundation for our opposition to slavery—and not just any religion will do. David Brion Davis notes that when, in the 1840s, British civil servants told the Turkish sultan in no uncertain terms that slavery had to be eliminated or there would be negative political consequences, Viscount Ponsonby, the ambassador to Turkey, reported that the message was heard "with extreme astonishment accompanied with a smile at a proposition for destroying an institution closely interwoven with the frame of society in this country, and intimately connected with the Law and with the habits and even the religion of all classes, from the Sultan himself down to the lowest peasant."[53] Davis puts it starkly: "Like algebra and knowledge of the Greek classics, racial slavery appears to have been one of the Arabs' contributions to Western civilization."[54] In a word, one must choose one's transcendental foundation very carefully.[55]

Thirdly, even if one arrives at absolute moral principles, *one must discover a way of interiorising genuine human dignity:* the heart will need to be

---

[52]   Cyrus H. Gordon, *Ugaritic Literature: A Comprehensive Translation of the Poetic and Prose Texts* (Rome: Pontificium Institutum Biblicum, 1949), p. 8.

[53]   Quoted in Davis, *Slavery and Human Progress (op. cit.)*, p. 302.

[54]   David Brion Davis, *Religion, Moral Values, and Our Heritage of Slavery* (New Haven, Conn.: Yale University Press, 2001), p. 148.

[55]   Cf. Alvin J. Schmidt, *The Great Divide: The Failure of Islam and the Triumph of the West* (Boston, Mass.: Regina Orthodox Press, 2004), chap. 4 ("Slavery"), pp. 100-122.

changed, or one will not regard one's neighbour as oneself and enslave-ment of the neighbour will remain a live possibility. In one of the most pregnant interchanges in Jesus' ministry, the following dialogue took place:

> Then said Jesus to those Jews who believed in him, If you continue in my word, then you are my disciples indeed, and you shall know the truth, and the truth shall set you free.
>
> They answered him, We are Abraham's seed, and were never in bond-age to anyone: how do you say, You shall be made free?
>
> Jesus answered them, Verily, verily, I say to you, Whosoever commits sin is the slave to sin—and the slave does not remain in the house forever; but the Son abides forever. If the Son therefore shall make you free, you will be free indeed.[56]

Jesus' hearers, ironically, were in hopeless bondage to the Romans, who had subjugated Israel and would, in A.D. 70, destroy the Temple and cause the dispersion of the Jewish people for millennia. But their immediate problem was their lack of recognition that their worse slavery followed from their own self-centredness. They needed changed hearts—which Jesus offered to them as an entirely free gift. It is that transformation which alone can provide the essential motivation to give up slaving prac-tices. No philosophy, ideology, or humanistic panacea can achieve this—and without it all the moralistic rhetoric in the world will achieve little, as past history has abundantly demonstrated.

Finally, *one must see the larger picture.* Slavery is but one affront to hu-man dignity. Its basic error is not to recognise the humanity of all those who benefit from the same genetic-chromosomal nature. Slavery refuses to treat genuine human beings as such; it reduces them to things, to chat-tel. This is precisely what occurs in other realms, and we must see the pattern, so that we do not engage in limited crusades instead of fighting the problem at its core.

When legal philosopher Ronald Dworkin's book, *Life's Dominion,* was published, the author gave a public lecture, followed by discussion, in London. The argument of the book is that, owing to the need for the state to allow for religious differences, the civil law should stay clear of the abortion issue, since it is a religious matter (some arguing against it on the basis of their convictions, others arguing the other way according to their value-system). I posed the question: "Like the slave, the fetus satis-fies the entire genetic-chromosomal definition of a human being, but is

---

[56] John 8: 31-36.

incapable of defending his or her rights, including the right to life. I assume, therefore, on the basis of the argument in your book, that you would have stayed clear of the fight to emancipate the slaves and would have opposed efforts to legislate against slavery—since the acceptance or rejection of slavery likewise turns on conflicting ideological values?" Dworkin would not accept the logic of the analogy—overwhelming as it is—so, needless to say, my question did not receive a satisfactory reply.[57]

Fundamental moral questions are always interlocked. We must therefore fight modern variants of slavery with the clarity which comes from a transcendental perspective—and at the same time recognise the need simultaneously to battle against the multifarious parallel affronts to human dignity which mask as "choices" rather than what they really are: devices to reduce human persons to the status of means rather than ends.

---

[57] See John Warwick Montgomery, "New Light on the Abortion Controversy?," 60/7 New Oxford Review 24-26 (September 1993); Slaughter of the Innocents: Abortion, Birth Control and Divorce in Light of Science, Law and Theology (Westchester, Ill.: Crossway Books, 1981); and "Human Dignity in Birth and Death: A Question of Values," in his Christ Our Advocate (Bonn, Germany: Verlag für Kultur und Wissenschaft, 2002), pp. 153 ff. Cf. John Warwick Montgomery, "Evangelical Social Responsibility in Theological Perspective," in Gary Collins (ed.), Our Society in Turmoil (Carol Stream, Ill.: Creation House, 1970), pp. 13-23, 281-82.

SLAVERY IN THE OLD TESTAMENT, IN THE NEW TESTAMENT, AND TODAY

With special research on
"The Role of Evangelicals in the Abolition of Slavery"

Thomas Schirrmacher

I. The Term 'Slave' in the Old Testament

The term *slave* in Bible translations is given to misunderstanding, because it is all too easy to mistakenly read the cruel slavery of the Greeks, Romans, Muslims, Europeans, and Americans into the Old and New Testaments. For this reason, to describe what was allowed in the Bible, one should use terms other slave and rather speak of *bonded labour* (albeit only for real debts), *labour service,* or with Georg Huntemann speak of *servant-hood work.*[58] Alan Richardson has formulated it as follows:

> "The 'house-tables' deal with domestic slavery, not the criminal slavery of the galleys and mines. It should not be thought of in the light of modern slave-trading practices. Indeed, one must sympathize with the English translators in their efforts to render *doulos:* the 'servant' of the English Versions is too weak and colourless; the 'bond servant' of the Revised Version margin is accurate but archaic: while 'slave' is too apt to suggest to modern ears the inhumanities of *Uncle Tom's Cabin.* 'Workers' is perhaps the best modern rendering of *douloi,* even though it does not carry with it the suggestion of being tied to one's occupation and to one's employer."[59]

The Hebrew expression for slave, *'ebed* (pl. *'avadim)* is a direct derivation of the verb *'db,* which means 'to work:' consequently a *slave* is a simply a worker or a servant. The *'ebed* is distinguished from hired workers (*sakhir*) in three ways: he does not receive a salary for his work; he is a

---

[58] Georg Huntemann. *Biblisches Ethos im Zeitalter der Moralrevolution.* Hänssler: Neuhausen, 1996, p. 89. (Note explanatory statements as to why what was in the Old Testament was not slavery).

[59] Alan Richardson. *The Biblical Doctrine of Work.* SCM Press: London, 1952, p. 41. Luther's German translation used the word "servant" for the Greek word for slaves.

member of the household of his master (comp. Genesis 24:2; Leviticus 22:11 and below); and his Lord exercises a fatherly control over him . . ."[60]

The legal position of a slave/servant in Israel, over against the position of slaves among other peoples, was extraordinarily good. "The lot of slaves does not appear to have been particularly harsh."[61] *This is demonstrated in the fact that there is no word for 'slave,' but rather the same word that was used for 'worker.'* "The Bible uses the same word, *'ebed*, for servants as well as for slaves, such that it is often difficult to determine which meaning is meant in a particular section."[62]

In German the word *slave* (German *Sklave*) describes the misuse of the object. *Servant* is definitely a better rendering, which does more justice to the Old Testament institution. For that reason, the Jewish scholar Benno Jacob wants to completely dispel with the term slavery, because "A slave for a period of time is legal nonsense."[63] Good point

Leviticus 25:6 distinguishes between four dependent types of labour: the "manservant" (slave), the "maidservant," the "hired worker," and the "temporary resident."[64] In other passages there is a distinction made between the salaried "hired worker" and the "temporary resident" (both in Leviticus 22:10; 25:40).

2. Slaves' Rights in the Old Testament[65]

Even prior to the covenant at Sinai[66], one reads in Job 31: "If I have denied justice to my menservants and maidservants when they had a grievance

---

[60] H. H. C. "Slavery." cols. 1655-1660 in: *Encyclopedia Judaica*. vol. 14: Red-Sl. Enyclopedia Judaica: Jerusalem, 1971, here col. 1655 (emphasis excluded).

[61] "Slavery," p. 566 in: Isaac Landman (ed.). *The Universal Jewish Encyclopedia*. 10 vols. vol. 9. Universal Jewish Encyclopedia: New York, 1948; comp. ibid. on similar human slavery legislation in Talmudic Judaism (with additional literature) and H. H. C. "Slavery." op. cit., cols. 1657-1660.

[62] "Slavery," p. 566 in: Isaac Landman (ed.). *The Universal Jewish Encyclopedia*.

[63] B[enno] Jacob. *Auge um Auge: Eine Untersuchung zum Alten und Neuen Testament*. Philo Verlag: Berlin, 1929, p. 6.

[64] Comp. Hans Walter Wolff. *Anthropologie des Alten Testaments*. Chr. Kaiser: München, 1977³, p. 289.

[65] Comp. the comprehensive study from a historic-critical point of view Gregory C. Chirichigno. *Debt Slavery in Israel and the Ancient Near East*. Journal for the Study of the Old Testament, Supplement Series 141. Sheffield Academic Press: Sheffield (GB), 1993.

[66] I assume that the Book of Job reports from a time prior to or during Abraham's life; comp. on the justification Henry M. Morris. *The Remarkable Record of Job: The Ancient Wisdom, Scientific Accuracy, and Life-Changing Message of an Amazing Book*.

against me, what will I do when God confronts me? What will I answer when called to account? Did not he who made me in the womb make them? Did not the same one form us both within our mothers?"

There is a central social meaning to the fact that in the Sabbath commandment servants/slaves were also expressly freed from work for the day (Exodus 20:10; 23:12; comp. Deuteronomy 5:14-15). In the first form of the Ten Commandments one reads: "Remember the Sabbath day by keeping it holy. Six days you shall labour and do all your work, but the seventh day is a Sabbath to the LORD your God. On it you shall not do any work, neither you, nor your son or daughter, nor your manservant or maidservant, nor your animals, nor the alien within your gates. For in six days the Lord made the heavens and the earth, the sea, and all that is in them, but he rested on the seventh day. Therefore the LORD blessed the Sabbath day and made it holy."

In this context it should also be considered that in the Old Testament the masters of the slaves (as well as the rulers and the local masters) and their families always worked as well and that in the Bible, work is part of what makes up the dignity of a person. Gustav Warneck observes in this regard, ". . . Christian mission demonstrates via word and example that the brand of shame that is seen upon work due to slavery *rests upon a divine command . . .*"[67]

A slave/servant in the Old Testament was not a possession of his or her master without rights as was the case in Greek, Roman, Islamic or the varieties of modern colonial slavery[68]. Rather, the servant was a person with full rights in the presence of a judge. As Job made clear, this is the case because the servant is just as much created by God as every other person. Also, because the servant is an image of God, he or she may not be infringed upon (comp. 9:6). For this reason one reads: "If a man beats his male or female slave with a rod and the slave dies as a direct result, he must be punished . . ." (Exodus 21:20).

Baker Book House: Grand Rapids (MI), 1988; comp. my review in "Querschnitte" 4 (1991) 2: 17. Hans Möller. *Sinn und Aufbau des Buches Hiob.* Evangelische Verlagsanstalt: (Ost-)Berlin, 1955 defends the unity of the book against critical views.

[67] Gustav Warneck. *Die Stellung der evangelischen Mission zur Sklavenfrage.* C. Bertelsmann: Gütersloh, 1889, p. 67.

[68] Comp. on the history of slavery, above all modern slavery: Susanne Everett. *Geschichte der Sklaverei.* Bechtermünz Verlag: Augsburg, 1998 and Milton Meltzer. *Slavery: A World History.* Da Capo: New York, 1993 (revised edition in 2 vols. 1971 & 1972); abridged version for youth: Milton Meltzer. *All Times, All Peoples: A World History of Slavery.* Harper & Row: New York, 1980.

As John Murray presented rather fittingly, in the Bible the master does not own the slave/servant but rather his or her work.[69] For that reason a slave could have his own possessions (e.g., 1 Samuel 9:8; 2 Samuel 9:10, 12; 16:4; 19: 18). That was the only reason why, should the occasion arise, he was able to buy his own freedom, and indeed then, when he had to provide his own possessions as payment (Leviticus 25:29-30 would have applied to slaves).

Generally speaking, there were numerous protective measures relating to slaves/servants.[70] No master was to "rule ... ruthlessly," neither over slaves (Leviticus 25:43, 46) nor over hired workers (Leviticus 25:53); Exodus 21:1-11 has been titled "Regulations for the Protection of Slaves" in certain German translations.[71] Accordingly, an Israelite slave was to serve for six years at most (Exodus 21:2, also see Deuteronomy 15: 12, 18). If he wanted to offer lifelong service, the slave had to conclude an eternal covenant with his master (Deuteronomy 15:16-17). This condition demonstrates once again just how great the relationship of trust between master and servant could be. Israelite slavery could not have been so bad if people voluntarily expanded it through an agreement from six years to a lifelong arrangement.

A slave/servant was able to be corporally disciplined as one's own children were (which in Europe was also common with employees until around 1900), but if he suffered harm, for instance by losing an eye or a tooth, he had to be freed (Exodus 21:26-27). After the end of the period of slavery, the master had to give the slave/servant enough property so that he could establish his own existence: "And when you release him, do not send him away empty-handed. Supply him liberally from your flock, your threshing floor and your winepress. Give to him as the Lord your God has blessed you" (Deuteronomy 15:13-14). The reasoning, expressed next to the reminder that Israel was once itself oppressed as slaves, is of great importance (Deuteronomy 15:15): "Do not consider it a hardship to set your servant free, because his service to you these six years has been worth twice as much as that of a hired hand [that is, arguably, the profit gained and the salary saved]. And the Lord your God will bless you in everything you do" (Deuteronomy 15:18). The work of a slave is worth his wages. The wage consisted mostly in working off debts; however, it was

69   John Murray. *Principles of Conduct: Aspects of Biblical Ethics*. Wm. B. Eerdmans: Grand Rapids (MI), 1978 (1957 reprint), pp. 97-98.
70   Comp. Hans Walter Wolff. *Anthropologie des Alten Testaments*, pp. 290-295.
71   Revised Elberfelder translation.

also expressed in the form of a generous endowment to establish the slave's future.

Next to this there was a "right of redemption" (Leviticus 25:48) for slaves/servants, who had to be set free when they either bought their own freedom or when someone else bought their freedom (Leviticus 25:47-55). There even existed a "redemption duty" upon the "uncle" or the nephew, that is to say, the closest relatives ("his closest blood relative") (Leviticus 25:49).

This right of redemption shows that slavery was a state that always needed to be ended as soon as possible. Paul writes similarly: ". . . although if you can gain your freedom, do so" (1 Corinthians 7:21). Paul would never have been able to make such a statement about marriage and family which had been founded by God (". . . although if you can gain your freedom . . .").

A slave could be named as an heir, which as a rule occurred via adoption (e.g., Genesis 15:2-3[72]; 1 Chronicles 2:34-35[73]) and indeed not only in the case of childlessness, but rather also in the place of the biological heirs (Proverbs 17:2). Abraham had a servant Eliezer (Genesis 15:2), who was "the chief [or oldest] servant in his household" and was "in charge of all he had" (Genesis 24:2). What trust Abraham placed in his slave/servant! This servant of Abraham was charged with searching out a wife for Isaac, that is to say, of his future master (Genesis 24). Furthermore, the slave/servant could become an heir by marrying a daughter who was to receive an inheritance (1 Chronicles 2:35). *Complete upward mobility was possible for a slave.*

A slave/servant was circumcised (Genesis 17:12-13; Exodus 12:44) and with that action was completely accepted into the covenant with God. He took part in the Passover (Exodus 12:44) as well as in sacrifices and fellowship meals (Leviticus 22:11). He was to expressly rejoice in worship (Deuteronomy 12:12, 18; 16:11, 14).

One of the most astounding commands regarding the limitations on slavery is in Deuteronomy 23:15-16: "If a slave has taken refuge with you, do not hand him over to his master. Let him live among you wherever he likes and in whatever town he chooses. Do not oppress him." Hans Walter

---

[72] Comp. Carl F. Keil. *Genesis und Exodus.* Brunnen Verlag: Gießen, 1983⁴ (1878 reprint³), p. 222. That Abram says, "You have given me no children; so a servant in my household will be my heir" (Genesis 15:3) indicates that it is not biological offspring who will inherit but a servant born in the household.

[73] Comp. W. S. Bruce. *The Ethics of the Old Testament.* T. & T. Clark: Edinburgh, 1895, pp. 187-188.

Wolff writes in this connection: "This law is, as far as the ancient Orient is concerned, unique."[74]

Due to the fact that God wants men to be free, as Leviticus 25: 39-43 shows, slavery was not generally viewed positively: "If one of your countrymen becomes poor among you and sells himself to you, do not make him work as a slave. He is to be treated as a hired worker or a temporary resident among you; he is to work for you until the Year of Jubilee. Then he and his children are to be released, and he will go back to his own clan and to the property of his forefathers. Because the Israelites are my servants, whom I brought out of Egypt, they must not be sold as slaves. Do not rule over them ruthlessly, but fear your God." Slavery was to be avoided if at all possible. The poverty of a person was not to be exploited in order to bring him under a condition of slavery. For this reason, Amos strongly rebukes the selling of the poor (Amos 2:6). (Gentile slaves comprise the exception in Leviticus 25:44-46.)

With all of this I do not want to say that the Old Testament already understood the legal protections we have today in the 21st century for those employed and dependent. However, the Old Testament set itself apart from its surrounding environment as far as legal protection for dependent employees was concerned and was far ahead of its time in this morally sensitive area. In no case, in light of this legal protection, can a view be supported that says Old Testament slavery corresponded to later European and Islamic slavery. The way that Christian slave owners in the south of the USA used the Old Testament up into the 19th century was misguided and unjustified. If slave owners had held to the Old Testament, they would have had none of their slaves, alone for the very facts that the slaves were where they were as a result of robbery and were unable to become free.

3. Female Slaves in the Old Testament

The protective provisions for female slaves/maidservants with respect to marriage should be specifically outlined (Exodus 21:7-11). To this end I will borrow a section from my chapter on polygamy in my book *Ethics*. In that place I demonstrated that polygamy was tolerated in the Old Testament but was not regarded as the ideal, and that a number of passages, among them the following regarding maidservants, have been wrongly applied to polygamy.

---

[74]   Hans Walter Wolff. *Anthropologie des Alten Testaments*, p. 293.

Exodus 21:7-11

In my opinion the correct translation would literally read: "If someone sells his daughter as a [female] slave, she should not be treated like the [male] slaves. If she is not pleasing to her master, who will not take her for himself, he has to redeem her. He has no authority to sell her to a foreigner, because he has broken faith with respect to her. And in case he wants her for his son, he has to give her the rights a daughter has. If he marries another woman [in her place], he should not reduce her sustenance, clothing, and time [or oil]. If he does not provide her with these three things, she should move out for free, without any amount of money being paid" (Exodus 21:7-11).

It is not until one looks at the usual translation (excerpted) and interpretation that the problem becomes clear: "If she does not please the master who has selected her for himself, he must let her be redeemed. . . . If he selects her for his son, he must grant her the rights of a daughter. If he marries another woman, he must not deprive the first one of her food, clothing and marital rights. . . ."[75]

On the basis of this translation one assumes that what happens here is that a man takes a slave as a wife, that she later becomes displeasing to him, and that he takes another woman as an additional wife. In that case he should provide for her and not reduce the marital rights for the first wife if he marries a second.

To begin with, even if the passage were to have to do with polygamy, the passage says nothing about whether God allows polygamy. In the Old Testament there are many 'if-then' regulations, in which after the situation described as the 'if' in no way corresponds to the will of God.

In our passage it additionally hints that the initial situation is not desired by God, because the very reason the master should treat the slave well is because he has already broken faith with her (Exodus 21:8).

Admittedly the usual translation cannot clear up several problems. First of all, why does it have to do with the situation where the woman has been selected for someone (Exodus 21:9)? Why is there talk of the possibility of her freedom being purchased or of her having the right to move without their being any cost, if that is practically tantamount to divorce? What does the fact that the slave was intended for the son have to do with the marriage to a second woman? Does not everything speak for the idea that what is being addressed here is a case in which the mas-

---

[75]   In the German version this is the revised Elberfelder translation.

ter or his son has not married the slave, and where if one of them does not eventually marry her, she is still to be provided for and treated well?

The reasons for the first translation confirm this suspicion. There are three points, because of which another translation becomes necessary or possible.

1. A note in the quoted German Bible translation[76] notes that the translation in Exodus 21:8 "the master who has selected her for himself" is only found in 6 Hebrew manuscripts. In addition to that, there are the Greek Septuagint, the Aramaic Targum, and the Latin Vulgate. All other Hebrew manuscripts as well as Syrian, Persian, and Arabic translations have handed down a letter differently[77]: instead of "for himself" (Hebrew *lo* mit Wav), they read "not" (Hebrew *lo* mit Aleph). Instead of that it is therefore "who does not select her" and not "who selects her for himself." The master therefore does not marry the slave, but she should nevertheless be treated well because he has promised to marry her.

2. When in Exodus 21:8 it reads that "he marries another woman," this other woman has to be the first wife, since he does not marry the slave.

3. The translation of the word that is rendered "marital rights" (Hebrew *onata*) is taken solely from the context and from interpretation, since it appears only at this point in the Old Testament.[78] The basis for this translation is the Greek Septuagint, which renders the word with "her companionship" (Greek *homilia*). Admittedly the Greek word can also generally mean "contact," "association," "friendship" (in the New Testament it is otherwise only found in 1 Corinthians 15:33: "bad company"). The Hebrew word *onata* has been variously explained. In this way it has been derived from the "particular time" or draws parallels, as in Shalom Paul,[79] to old oriental texts. These texts contain the triad of "sustenance, clothing, and anointing" as the basis for life, whereby the oil stands for health. In any event the translation of "marital rights" is pure speculation, which, in my opinion, is derived from a false interpretation.

[76]   Ibid.
[77]   Comp. S. E. Dwight. *The Hebrew Wife.* op. cit., p. 15. According to Wilhelm Gesenius, E. Kautzsch. *Hebräische Grammatik.* Georg Olms: Hildesheim, 1962 (1909 reprint[28]), p. 313 (§ 103g) there are numerous passages in which the Masora in the Hebrew text calls for and has to call for exchanging the two words, so that in Exodus 21:8 a completely normal phenomenon is at issue.
[78]   A so-called *hapax legomenon.*
[79]   Shalom M. Paul. "Exod. 21:10 a Threefold Maintenance Clause." Journal of Near Eastern Studies 28 (1969): 48-53.

4. Releasing Slaves in the Old Testament

We have already become familiar with the right of redemption that a slave himself had, or that anyone else had who wanted to buy the slave's freedom.

The release of a slave was considered a good thing to do. The liberation of Israel from slavery in Egypt remained unforgotten, and it was simultaneously a liberation from spiritual slavery in Egypt as well as a liberation from the visible slavery of compulsory labour (e. g., Exodus 13:3, 14; 20:2; Deuteronomy 6:12; 7:8; 8:14; Psalm 81:6-8; Jeremiah 11:4; 34:13; Micah 6:4). This becomes particularly clear in the reasons provided for the protective regulations for slaves in Leviticus 25, as several excerpts will show: "Because the Israelites are my servants, whom I brought out of Egypt, they must not be sold as slaves. Do not rule over them ruthlessly . . ." (Leviticus 25:42-43); ". . . for the Israelites belong to me as servants. They are my servants, whom I brought out of Egypt. I am the Lord your God" (Leviticus 25:55).

Freeing a slave was above all called for when the reason for the enslavement was unjust: "Is not this the kind of fasting I have chosen: to loose the chains of injustice and untie the cords of the yoke, to set the oppressed free and break every yoke?" (Isaiah 58:6). The actual year to set free was the Year of Jubilee. (Jesus quoted this text in Luke 4:16-22 together with Isaiah 61:1 et seq. at one of his first public appearances and proclaims that the fulfilment of the year of freedom had begun with him.)

The most comprehensive chapters having to do with proclaiming freedom are found in Jeremiah and Nehemiah. In Jeremiah 34:8-22 a "covenant" (mentioned repeatedly in 34:8-22) was made under King Zedekiah to release all slaves in the course of the Year of Jubilee, that is to say, to "proclaim 'freedom'" (Jeremiah 34:17). When the "leaders" take back their slaves, their sin brings God's anger on them (Jeremiah 34:19-22). In the process God expressly reminds them of his law of the Year of Jubilee (Jeremiah 34:14-15, 17) and of the liberation of Israel from Egyptian slavery (Jeremiah 34:13).

Alongside this there were times slaves were set free when it was not the Year of Jubilee, such as the second Old Testament report of a large-scale release of slaves shows. Nehemiah 5 reports a major action to forgive debt by the wealthy, by which many slaves were given their freedom and additional people were prevented from becoming slaves.

In summary, one can say the following: The Jews "differentiate themselves from all peoples of antiquity ... in that they had the most highly advanced protective legislation for slaves."[80]

5. The Death Penalty for Slave Thieves and Slave Traders

How did one (legally) become a slave/servant in the Old Testament? There was no situation where it was legal to bring someone into slavery through theft or through sale. The death penalty was the punishment for such actions: "Anyone who kidnaps another and either sells him or still has him when he is caught must be put to death" (Exodus 21:16).[81] "If a man is caught kidnapping one of his brother Israelites and treats him as a slave or sells him, the kidnapper must die. You must purge the evil from among you" (Deuteronomy 24:7). **Alone this instruction condemns Greek, Roman, Islamic, and the varieties of modern colonial slavery. Practically all the blacks in North and South America were made into slaves by abduction. The slave traders and their financiers in genteel banking houses and aristocratic families assaulted the lives of others and thus, according to Old Testament law, forfeited their own lives.**

Gary North points out correctly that this did not only apply to the brutal slave hunters, but rather also to the respectable English and American citizens who financed the slave trade.[82]

Michael Parsons writes: "It should be emphasized that the New Testament writers did not overlook the errors of slavery. The Pauline list of lawbreakers includes slave traders (1 Timothy 1:9-10). John includes slavery in his analysis of the errors which permeated Babylon, whereby the city would be judged (Revelation 18:13)."[83]

---

[80]   Elisabeth Herrmann-Otto. *Sklaverei und Freilassung in der griechisch-römischen Welt.* Hildesheim. Georg Olms, 2009, p. 203, in detail pp. 203-209.

[81]   Comp. Rousas J. Rushdoony. *Institutes of Biblical Law.* Presbyterian and Reformed: Phillipsburg, 1973, pp. 484-488; Gary North. *Victim's Rights: The Biblical View of Civil Justice.* Institute for Christian Economics: Tyler (TX), 1990, pp. 65-84.

[82]   Ibid., p. 79.

[83]   Michael Parsons. "Slavery and the New Testament: Equality and Submissiveness." *Vox Evangelica* 18 (1988): 89-96, here p. 90.

6. How did an Individual become a Slave according to the Old Testament?

Let us return to Old Testament slavery. How did someone (legally) become a slave according to the Old Testament?

A person could become a slave by obligating oneself to remain a slave for life (Exodus 21:5-6) or by being born as a slave (Genesis 15:3; 17:12-13, 27; Exodus 23:12; Leviticus 22:11; Genesis 14:14). Both, however, presupposed already existing slavery. This also applied to the purchase of non-Israelite slaves (Leviticus 25:44-45; Genesis 17:12-13, 27; 37:28-36; 39:1). Here the issue is likewise the sale of slaves who in some other manner had become slaves. Normally only the following individuals could (involuntarily) become slaves/servants:

1. **Prisoners of War** (Numbers 31:7-12; Deuteronomy 20:10-14; 21:10-14; Genesis 14:21). According to Deuteronomy 20:11, Israel always had to first offer peace to a besieged city, which then meant "forced labour," that is, slavery with all its associated rights. If peace were to be refused, they came down on the city with the ban. Given this situation, slavery was therefore an act of grace. This type of slavery is no longer possible in New Testament times, because, I believe, God no longer gives any people the command to come down upon a people with the ban.

2. **Individuals unable to pay debts.** Here lies the focal point of slavery. In slavery one serves to work off what one owes to another, so that one can also speak of "debt servant-hood."[84] In this case a person could resort to putting himself into a position of slavery (Leviticus 25:39-55; Deuteronomy 15:12-15; comp. Exodus 21:2-6) or give his children over into slavery (Exodus 21:7-11; Nehemiah 5:5) and then also, of course, to redeem his family and himself. In 2 Kings 4:1 a "creditor" takes two sons of a woman as slaves. *However, the process of slavery was not only a burden but also social welfare for an individual who for no fault of his own goes bankrupt.* "As elsewhere in the old Orient, slavery attributable to debts, in which the family would then get involved, was not actually a penalty; rather, it was civil law compensation to the creditor from the debtor for his inability to pay."[85]

This Old Testament system must not be confused with the most common type of slavery in present times, debt servant-hood. Nowadays debts

---

[84] Paul Volz. *Die Biblischen Altertümer*. Fourier: Wiesbaden, 1989 (1914 reprint), p. 505.

[85] J. Scharbert. "Strafe: II. Biblisch." col. 1099 in: Josef Höfer, Karl Rahner et al. (eds.). *Lexikon für Theologie und Kirche*. 14. vols. Herder: Freiburg, 1986[St]. vol. 9.

are wrongfully caused and cannot be repaid, for instance when fictitious user fees for tools in India exceed wages. In the Old Testament we are dealing with real debts which have to be duly paid off or worked off.

3. **Criminal Offenders.** In addition to the aforesaid, an individual unable to pay his debts could above all be placed into slavery by a **court order.**[86] Insofar as criminal offenses are concerned, slavery fulfilled the function that financial penalties and imprisonment should have today. This applied especially for thieves (Exodus 22:1-3; Leviticus 25:40). Exodus 22:2 reads as follows: "A thief must certainly make restitution, but if he has nothing, he must be sold to pay for his theft."

7. Slavery in the New Testament

There have been many who have stumbled over the fact that the New Testament asks slaves/servants to work particularly well and honestly for their masters (e.g., Titus 2:9-11; Ephesians 6:5-9; Colossians 3:22-4:1; 1 Timothy 6:1-2; 1 Peter 2:18-25; 1 Corinthians 7:21-24). However, the justification is important: "... not only when their eye is on you and to win their favour, but with sincerity of heart and reverence for the Lord. Whatever you do, work at it with all your heart, as working for the Lord, not for men ..." (Colossians 3:22). It is not the payer of the wages who is the actual employer; rather, it is God! The slave knows that in God's eyes his work is good and worthy. Was this type of request to work to the tastes of the masters? Hardly.

Additionally, the New Testament turns against the slave trade. Let us repeat the statement by Michael Parsons: "It should be highlighted that the New Testament writers do not overlook the mistake of slavery. The Pauline list of lawbreakers includes 'slave traders' (1 Timothy 1:9-10). John includes slavery in his analysis of errors that pervade Babylon, and these are errors whereby the state is judged (Revelation 18:13)."[87]

The sharp admonitions that were given to masters can only be understood if based on this basic attitude. The admonitions reminded the masters of their lawful responsibilities, because God does not look at a person's standing: "Anyone who does wrong will be repaid for his wrong,

---

[86] So also H. H. C. "Slavery." op. cit., col. 1655; comp. Gordon Wenham. "Law and the Legal System in the Old Testament," pp. 24-52 in: Bruce Kaye, Gordon Wenham (eds.). *Law, Morality and the Bible*. Inter-Varsity Press: Leicester, 1978, here pp. 43-45.

[87] Michael Parsons. "Slavery and the New Testament: Equality and Submissiveness." *Vox Evangelica 18* (1988): 89-96, here p. 90.

and there is no favouritism. Masters, provide your slaves with what is right and fair, because you know that you also have a Master in heaven" (Colossians 3:25 – 4:1).

The same Paul who encouraged slaves to work well and to prove their Christian faith as slaves was able to write: "Each one should remain in the situation which he was in when God called him. Were you a slave when you were called? Don't let it trouble you—**although if you can gain your freedom, do so.** For he who was a slave when he was called by the Lord is the Lord's freedman; similarly, he who was a free man when he was called is Christ's slave" (1 Corinthians 7:20-22). In Philemon Paul vehemently engages himself for the freedom of a slave.[88] Is that a contradiction? No.

There is another translation of the passage that is now generally viewed as wrong – "even if you can become free, rather stay all the more" – and it is often viewed as the reigning view of the early church. Alphons Steinmann, however, demonstrated as early as 1917[89] that to think that only in modern times there was a desire for slaves to see freedom is false, since this view can also be found in scores of church fathers and theologians across the centuries.

In the Bible mankind is a slave of sin and is caught in rebellion against God. If he accepts that God is justified in his judgment and accepts the substitutionary, sacrificial death of Jesus Christ, he is one who is called by God. Forgiveness of sins is what frees that individual to experience a new life. Not all external, life circumstances have to immediately take a turn for the good in order to have this new life with God. Even as a slave a person can wholeheartedly serve God. It has absolutely nothing to do with whether one finds slavery agreeable or justifiable. Paul clearly recommends the emancipation of slaves and even fights for it. However, belief in God reprioritizes one's values. It is not work that makes life valuable, but rather the Creator and Redeemer who gives the work. The penetrating power of Christianity consists in the fact that by pointedly calling upon the righteousness of God, there is a call for and promotion of righteousness; and even then when this is withheld, in thankfulness towards God, the call continues and does not make itself dependent on external

---

[88]   Comp. Herbert M. Carson. *The Epistle of Paul to the Colossians and Philemon.* The Tyndale New Testament Commentary. Wm. B. Eerdmans: Grand Rapids (MI), 1979 (1960 reprint). In part. pp. 21-24.

[89]   Alphons Steinmann. "Zur Geschichte der Auslegung von 1Kor 7,21." *Theologische Revue* 16 (1917): 340-348.

circumstances. Internal freedom can and should precede external freedom.

To repeat: The Old Testament sharply condemns slavery as we know it from Greek, Roman, Islamic, or from modern, colonial history. It imposes the death penalty on human traffickers, and the New Testament follows this condemnation (see the passages above).

8. Slavery and Christians: From the early Church to Abolition

It is no coincidence that the early church unsettled the Roman world and Hellenistic civilization, in which slavery was an inherent part of the structure of society.[90] It did this when it began to make it possible for slaves to have complete participation in their congregations and when it set slaves free or bought their freedom on a large scale.[91]

"With the demand for equality before God, which always taught Christians to see in other Christians only another individual with whom one was a slave of the Lord, the lowest standing became the standing of the Christian."[92]

"Slaves were even able to become clerics, indeed even bishops."[93] The most famous example is Bishop Kallist (d. 222 A.D.), who went from slavery to become the highest representative of the church as Bishop of Rome.[94] "All the Roman bishops up to Victor I (189-198) may very well have been former slaves or Orientals."[95] Freeing slaves counted in the

---

[90]   Comp. Elisabeth Herrmann-Otto. *Sklaverei und Freilassung in der griechisch-römischen Welt.* Hildesheim. Georg Olms, 2009; Stefan Knoch. *Sklavenfürsorge im Römischen Reich: Formen und Motive.* Hildesheim: Georg Ohlms, 2009; Elisabeth Hermann-Otto (ed.). *Unfreie Arbeits- und Lebensverhältnisse von der Antike bis in die Gegenwart: Eine Einführung.* Hildesheim: Georg Ohlms, 2009.

[91]   Comp. Henneke Gülzow. "Soziale Gegebenheiten der altkirchlichen Mission," pp. 227-243 in: Heinzgünter Frohnes, Uwe W. Knorr (eds.). *Die Alte Kirche. Kirchengeschichte als Missionsgeschichte* 1. Chr. Kaiser: München, 1974, here pp. 207-208.

[92]   Hennecke Gülzow. *Christentum und Sklaverei in den ersten drei Jahrhunderten.* Rudolf Habelt: Bonn, 1969, p. 173.

[93]   Adolf von Harnack. *Die Mission und Ausbreitung des Christentums in den ersten drei Jahrhunderten.* VMA-Verlag: Wiesbaden, o. J. (1924 reprint⁴), p. 193.

[94]   His life is presented in Hennecke Gülzow. *Christentum und Sklaverei in den ersten drei Jahrhunderten.* op. cit., pp. 146-172.

[95]   Johannes Neumann. " Bischof I: Das katholische Bischofsamt," pp. 653-682 in: Gerhard Krause, Gerhard Müller (eds.). *Theologische Realenzyklopädie.* vol. 6. Walter de Gruyter: Berlin, 1980, p. 659.

early church as a good work, Christians were publicly engaged in efforts relating to the destiny of slaves,[96] and slaves had full rights in the church.[97] (It is to be pointed out at this juncture that slavery in antiquity differed from later Islamic and then from 'Christian' slavery in that being set free and the purchase of freedom [also by the slave himself] were both possible.)[98]

Gary North quotes William L. Westermann's question in his investigation of Greek and Roman slavery as to why it was specifically Christianity that abolished slavery in the long run.[99] His answer is that slavery actually found its end in Christ on the cross but that it was only in the course of the development of the Christian church that it grew in its realization.[100] This view is not to be dismissed. The Christian faith has made several contributions to history within and outside of the Christian world that are not traceable back to an expressed biblical command or prohibition. Examples include work-free time on weekends, the end of the degradation of women, the prohibition against child-labour, and all the regulations that arise from the view of equality that sees human beings as made in the image of God, such as the abolition of slavery.

North wants to demonstrate that slavery is a component of the year of Jubilee and for that reason it found an end every 50 years.[101] Since Jesus Christ saw himself as the fulfilment of the Year of Jubilee and proclaimed a permanent Jubilee Year (both Luke 4:17-19 and 21), slavery and bonded servitude were abolished, even if they were not forbidden in the their biblical form, and even if it took some time until this salvific truth prevailed in Christianity.

---

[96] See Hennecke Gülzow. *Christentum und Sklaverei in den ersten drei Jahrhunderten.* op. cit., pp. 173-176.

[97] Adolf von Harnack. *Die Mission und Ausbreitung des Christentums in den ersten drei Jahrhunderten.* op. cit., pp. 192-195. Hennecke Gülzow. *Christentum und Sklaverei in den ersten drei Jahrhunderten.* op. cit., pp. 76-146 looks at the question of slavery in detail in early Christian documents and churches on the basis of the few available sources.

[98] See in this connection in particular Elisabeth Herrmann-Otto. *Sklaverei und Freilassung in der griechisch-römischen Welt.* Hildesheim. Georg Olms, 2009.

[99] Gary North. *Tools of Dominion: The Case Laws of Exodus.* Institute for Christian Economics: Tyler (TX), 1990, p. 186. Also William L. Westermann. *The Slave Systems of Greek and Roman Antiquity.* American Philosophical Society: Philadelphia (USA), 1955, p. 159.

[100] Gary North. *Tools of Dominion.* op. cit., pp. 186-187.

[101] Gary North. "The Jubilee Year and Abolitionism." *Biblical Economics Today* 11 (1988) 2 (Feb/Mar): 1-4.

Even if it was the case that the end of slavery was achieved prior to the end of the 19th century, it was something that had always been disputed among theologians and legal experts[102] – completely in contrast to Islam, which will be treated in more detail in Section 10.

"The Synod of Châlons in France declared the following in 650 A.D.: 'The highest piety and religion demands that Christianity be completely freed from the chains of slavery.' In 922 A.D. the Koblenz Synod in the East Frankish Empire came to the resolution that the sale of a Christian was to be considered murder."[103]

The first legal book in history to reject servitude and – a fortiori – slavery is the *Sachsenspiegel* (literal English translation is 'Saxon Mirror'), dated 1235 A.D. It was composed by Eike Repgow. In it the lack of freedom is seen as an injustice which by practice of habit comes to be seen as just. Jesus' teaching on paying taxes to Caesar indicates that a coin belongs to the person whose picture it bears; since man bears God's image, he belongs to God and no one else."[104]

The discussion of the conquest of the Indians in Latin America is notable. In the surrounding discussion, the Pope – unsuccessfully – spoke out for the human dignity of the Indians and against their enslavement.[105]

On account of this, it was only consistent for Protestant world missions and missionaries such as David Livingstone or Elias Schrenk to engage in massive efforts to end the slave trade and slavery.[106] This slavery

---

[102] Comp. Alvin J. Schmidt. *Wie das Christentum die Welt veränderte.* Gräfelfing: Dr. Ingo Resch, 2009, pp. 325-348 (where the complexity of the topic is also well presented); for antiquity Elisabeth Herrmann-Otto. *Sklaverei und Freilassung in der griechisch-römischen Welt.* Hildesheim. Georg Olms, 2009, pp. 209-214; for the 17th century Bernd Francke. *Sklaverei und Unfreiheit im Naturrecht des 17. Jahrhunderts.* Hildesheim: Georg Ohlms, 2009.

[103] Egon Flaig. *Weltgeschichte der Sklaverei.* op. cit., p. 157.

[104] Ibid., p. 158.

[105] Egon Flaig. *Weltgeschichte der Sklaverei.* op. cit., pp. 164-165; Thomas Schirrmacher. *Rassismus.* Hänssler: Holzgerlingen, 2009, p. 59; Matthias Gillner. *Bartolomé de Las Casas und die Eroberung des indianischen Kontinents. Theologie und Frieden 12.* Stuttgart: Kohlhammer, 1997.

[106] Comp. Gustav Warneck. Die *Stellung der evangelischen Mission zur Sklavenfrage.* C. Bertelsmann: Gütersloh, 1889; Chapter "The Spiritual Warfare Against Slavery," pp. 204-224 in: Timothy L. Smith. *Revivalism and Social Reform in Mid-Nineteenth-Century America.* Abingdon Press: New York, 1957 and as practical examples Al. Michelsen. "Der Sklavenhandel Ostafrica's." *Allgemeine Missions-Zeitschrift* 2 (1875): 518-527 and 3 (1876): 335-348+383-392; Theodor Arndt. "Was können wir deutschen Protestanten zur Unterdrückung des Sclavenhandels in Afrika tun?"

had absolutely nothing to do with what was allowed in the Old Testament. Missionary societies and British Evangelicals were also significantly involved in the abolition of slavery.[107] If anything it is to be borne in mind "that the anti-slavery movement in the 18th and 19th centuries did not primarily take its argumentation and inspiration from human rights convictions but rather above all from religious beliefs and convictions."[108] But let us start a bit earlier.[109] While African peoples had long enslaved each other,[110] and things had so developed that Arab princes had

---

Protestantische Kirchenzeitung für das evangelische Deutschland Nr. 16 dated April 17, 1889: cols. 375-382; "Sklaverei und Sklavenhandel II." *Neue Evangelische Kirchenzeitung Nr. 19* (1877) 45 (November 10, 1877): 718.

[107] Comp. Jonathan Hildebrandt. *History of the Church in Africa*. Africa Christian Press: Achimota (Ghana), 1981, pp. 7-79; Garth Lean. Wilberforce: *Lehrstück christlicher Sozialreform. Theologie und Dienst 3.* Brunnen Verlag: Gießen, 1974. Walter Bienert. *Der überholte Marx.* Evangelisches Verlagswerk: Stuttgart, 1974[2], pp. 96-110 correctly resist the accusation that Christianity was to blame for slavery.

[108] Jozef Punt. *Die Idee der Menschenrechte: Ihre geschichtliche Entwicklung und ihre Rezeption durch die moderne katholische Sozialverkündigung. Abhandlungen zur Sozialethik 26.* F. Schöningh: Paderborn, 1987, p. 168 (with additional literature); comp. on the history of the abolition of slavery Susanne Everett. *Geschichte der Sklaverei.* Bechtermünz Verlag: Augsburg, 1998, pp. 194-245 and on the fight of Bible believing Christians against slavery comp. Victor B. Howard. *The Evangelical War Against Slavery and Caste: The Life and Times of John G. Fee.* Associated University Press: Cranbury (NJ) & London, 1996; Howard Temperley. *British Antislavery 1833-1870.* Logman: London, 1972 (on the Christian argumentation against Slavery see pp. 14-15).

[109] Comp. on the history of slavery Christian Delacampagne. *Die Geschichte der Sklaverei.* Wiss. Buchges.: Darmstadt, 2004; Egon Flaig. *Weltgeschichte der Sklaverei.* München: C. H. Beck, 2009; Susanne Everett. *Geschichte der Sklaverei.* Bechtermünz: Augsburg, 1998; especially on the USA: Jochen Meissner et al. *Schwarzes Amerika: Eine Geschichte der Sklaverei.* C. H. Beck: München, 2008; John Hope Franklin, Alfred A. Moss. *Von der Sklaverei zur Freiheit: Die Geschichte der Schwarzen in den USA.* Ullstein: Berlin, 1999; Hugh Thomas. *The Slave Trade: The History of the Atlantic Slave Trade: 1440-1870.* London: Phoenix Books, 2006; Harm Mögenburg, Heinz-Peter Rauckes. *Sklaverei und Dreieckshandel: Menschen als Ware.* Diesterweg: Frankfurt, 1988; 1996 (paperback) and my book *Rassismus.* Hänssler: Holzgerlingen, 2009.

[110] According to Tidiane N'Diaye. *Der verschleierte Völkermord.* op. cit., p. 32-33 the thesis that as a consequence black African society was not familiar with servitude or forced labor is difficult to maintain. From time immemorial there was also a system of servitude in Africa. There were two categories of subjects: house slaves (or slaves of the crown) and the much harder working field servant, whose fate was in fact everything other than enviable. Those who achieved the

become the masters of the African slave trade (see in this connection the more comprehensive Section 10), European involvement began in 1444 when a Portuguese expedition unloaded 235 slaves from Mauritius in Lagos. It was in 1510 that for the first time 50 black slaves were brought from Spain to Haiti in order to work in the silver mines, and it was in 1619 that for the first time slaves were brought to the land which is now the USA.

The transatlantic slave trade was born,[111] which was a business triangle in which cheap goods, hard liquor, and weapons from Europe, through the inclusion of Arab slave traders, were often exchanged for slaves from Europe and these then exchanged for American colonial goods. With this it was taken for granted that there would be a social and physical death of a portion of the slaves, since slaves were valued and treated as goods. Between 1450 and 1900 it is estimated that 11.7 million slaves from Africa were carried off to the Americas. Of this total, 9.8 million actually found America to be their country of destination. Between 1 and 2 million slaves died during what was approximated to be 50,000 passages.[112]

9. The Role of Evangelicals in the Abolition of Slavery

From one day to the next, the British let go of 800,000 slaves in 1834.[113] How did this happen?

In addition to other economic and social factors, Evangelical Revivalism was significantly involved in bringing an end to slavery. Indeed it is at this point that the designation *Evangelicals* came about in the first place.[114] This applies to the legal abolition of slavery in Great Britain as well as to the anti-slavery movement in the USA.[115]

---

status of house slave did so either by being designated as such by a lord or through marriage.

[111] Comp. I part. Christian Delacampagne. *Die Geschichte der Sklaverei.* op. cit., pp. 112-124.

[112] Comp. Jochen Meissner, Ulrich Mücke, Klaus Weber. *Schwarzes Amerika: Eine Geschichte der Sklaverei.* Bundeszentrale für politische Bildung: Bonn, 2008.

[113] Seymour Drescher. *Abolition.* op. cit., p. 265.

[114] The most important literature on the role of Evangelicals in the anti-slavery movement **in Great Britain:** Roger Anstey. *The Atlantic Slave Trade and British Abolition 1760-1810: The Story of the First American Revolution for Negro Rights.* Atlantic Highlands (NJ): Humanities Press, 1975; J. R. Oldfield. *Popular Politics and British Anti-Slavery: The Mobilisation of Public Opinion against the Slave Trade, 1787 - 1807.* London: Routledge, 1998; Christopher Leslie Brown. *Moral Capital: Foundations of*

It was in 1688 that Quakers in England and the USA first demanded that all slaves be released. By 1780 all Quakers had released their slaves.[116] George Whitefield und John Wesley, who set "Methodist" revivalism in motion in England and the USA, fought vehemently against the "sin" of slavery. Wesley published his book *Thoughts upon Slavery* in 1774. Beginning in 1784, slave owners were excommunicated by Methodists. In England many friends of Wesley who were involved in politics became active in opposition to slavery. The most famous of these is William Wilberforce (1759-1833).[117]

British Abolitionism. Chapel Hill (NC): Univ. of North Carolina Press, 2006, in particular "British Evangelicals and Caribbean Slavery after the American War" pp. 333-390 and "The Society of Friends and the Antislavery Identity," pp. 391-450; Eric Metaxas. *Amazing Grace: William Wilberforce and the Heroic Campaign to End Slavery*. New York: HarperCollins Publisher, 2007 (unfortunately without footnotes); **in the USA**: Gilbert Hobbs Barnes. *The Anti-Slavery Impulse: 1830-1844*. New York (NY): Harcourt, Brace, 1964; Mark. A. Noll. *Das Christentum in Nordamerika. Kirchengeschichte in Einzeldarstellungen 4*. Leipzig: Evangelische Verl.-Anstalt, 2000, pp. 114, 121-123; Donald G. Matthews. *Slavery And Methodism: A Chapter in American Morality 1780-1845*. Princeton (NJ): Princeton University Press, 1965, pp. 3-28 (on the Methodist split in the USA over the question of slavery; also John Wolffe on this topic. *The Expansion of Evangelicalism*, op. cit., pp. 210-211); **on Great Britain and the USA together**: Seymour Drescher. *Abolition: A History of Slavery and Antislavery*. Cambridge: Cambridge University Press, 2009, pp. 205-241; Alvin J. Schmidt. *Wie das Christentum die Welt veränderte*. Gräfelfing: Dr. Ingo Resch, 2009, pp. 325-348; Egon Flaig. *Weltgeschichte der Sklaverei*. op. cit., pp. 199-201.

[115] S. Dave Unander. *Shattering the Myth of Race: Genetic Realities and Biblical Truths*. Judson Press: Valley Forge (PA, USA), 2000, pp. 24-26, 36-40.

[116] Comp. to the leading role of the Quakers in Great Britain and the USA and their dominant role in the first anti-slavery committee in John Wolffe. *The Expansion of Evangelicalism*. op. cit., pp. 198-199; Roger Anstey. *The Atlantic Slave Trade and British Abolition 1760-1810*. op. cit., pp. 200-235 (chapter "Origins of Quaker Action Against the Slave Trade"); Christopher Leslie Brown. *Moral Capital: Foundations of British Abolitionism*. Chapel Hill (NC): Univ. of North Carolina Press, 2006, in particular "The Society of Friends and the Antislavery Identity," pp. 391-450.

[117] Comp. regarding Wilberforce, John White. "Christian Responsibility to Reform Society: the Example of William Wilberforce and the Clapham Sect." *Evangelical Review of Theology 32* (2008) 2: 166-172; John Wolffe. *The Expansion of Evangelicalism: The Age of Wilberforce, More, Chalmers and Finney*. Downers Grove (IL): InterVarsity Press, 2007, pp. 159-227; Chuck Stetson (ed.). *Creating the Better Hour*. Macon (GA): Striud & Hall, 2007; Eric Metaxas. *Amazing Grace: William Wilberforce and the Heroic Campaign to End Slavery*. op. cit., (unfortunately without footnotes). Wilberforce's evangelical theology is expressed best in his work *William Wilberforce. Real Christianity*. Portland (OR): Multnomah Press, 1982.

In addition to William Wilberforce, the long underrated Thomas Clarkson[118] should be mentioned.[119] Additionally, the former slave trader John Newton, who wrote a book against the slave trade[120] as well as the "national an-
them" of the anti-slavery movement, "Amazing Grace," is also noteworthy.

The abolition of slavery was carried out by religious fanatics against
Modernism, which had pointed to the priority of economic concerns and
found that it had to bow to the reality of moral concerns. "Human rights
developed in the fight against slavery."[121] "Thus it was not enlightened and
revolutionary France but rather pious England that brought about the end
of slavery."[122] Egon Flaig writes that this "is indebted to the longest and
most intensive fight for the liberation of mankind. Those who carried on
this battle are not to be found in Enlightenment philosophy; where one
makes a find is in the spiritual realm of Protestant minorities ..."[123]

"That scientific racism, which expressly or tacitly assumes polygene-
sis, was not able to establish itself until the second half of the 19th century, lies primarily in a strong Evangelical movement that was present
there and whose followers believed that all people descended from Adam.
... The ethnological discourse in France was able to develop without any
influence from a Protestant Evangelicalism and for that reason took a
more radical turn than in Great Britain or even in the United States."[124]

It was in the 1830's at the latest that an increasing number of Evangelicals in the northern United States became active in the abolitionist
movement. *Uncle Tom's Cabin* (1852) is the most outstanding example. The
book was written by the daughter of the famous Evangelical revivalist
preacher Lyman Beecher. And it was not even the most radical book
against slavery by Harriet Elizabeth Beecher Stowe (1811-1896), even if
was by far the most successful.[125] The South – admittedly also due to its

---

[118] See in particular J. R. Oldfield. *Popular Politics and British Anti-Slavery*. op. cit., pp.
       70-95.
[119] John Wolffe. *The Expansion of Evangelicalism*. op. cit., p. 200 on the dispute be-
       tween Wilberforce's sons and Thomas Clarkson on who was more important.
[120] John Newton. *Thoughts Upon the African Slave Trade*. London: J. Buckland and J.
       Johnson, 1788.
[121] Egon Flaig. *Weltgeschichte der Sklaverei*. München: C. H. Beck, 2009, p. 11.
[122] Arnold Angenendt. *Toleranz und Gewalt: Das Christentum zwischen Bibel und Schwert*.
       Münster: Aschendorff, 2008⁴, p. 225.
[123] Egon Flaig. Weltgeschichte der Sklaverei. op. cit., pp. 199-200.
[124] George M. Fredrickson. *Rassismus: Ein historischer Abriß*. Hamburger Edition:
       Hamburg, 2004, pp. 69-70.
[125] Additional books by Ellen J. Goldner. "Stowe, Harriet Beecher," pp. 101-102 in:
       Encyclopedia of Race and Racism. Vol. 3. Detroit: Thomason Gale, 2008.

Catholic dominance which was made co-responsible for slavery – became the embodiment of the (enslaving) anti-Christ. "Evangelical abolitionists developed the doctrine of 'higher law,' a law that was higher than the United States Constitution. What was meant was a peculiarly vague mixture of biblical and natural rights-philanthropic arguments,"[126] which justified a right to resist slavery. However, as a general rule, there was no violence perpetrated by Evangelicals, as was the case with other abolitionist powers. The Evangelicals were rather in favour of secession. According to Hochgeschwender, of the 1218 violent disturbances that have been shown to have occurred between 1828 and 1861, there were only eleven that can be traced back to Evangelicals. For this reason, Egon Flaig begins the chapter "The Fight for the Abolition of Slavery" with the section "Evangelical Abolitionism. The first Prohibitions."[127]

Alvon J. Schmidt estimates that in the USA two-thirds of the anti-slavery movement consisted of Evangelicals.[128] Jochen Meissner writes "that the Evangelical-sectarian origins of many European settlements in the territory of the present day USA offered fertile ground for the spread of ideas which condemned slavery."[129] He continues:

"Part of the abolition movement became radical in the 1830s in the north and won new advocates in the printer (and publicist) William Lloyd Garrison (1805-1879) or in Evangelicals, such as Theodore Weld. Garrison published *The Liberator* in Boston (1831-1865), which declared slavery to be a sin and campaigned against its reform and against financial compensation for slaveholders. Instead, it advocated the immediate abolition of slavery. Weld (1803-1895) also supported the immediate abolition of slavery. He composed influential pamphlets on the topic – *The Bible Against Slavery* (1837) and *American Slavery As It Is* (1839). The latter is supposed to have been the most read anti-slavery document read next to Stowe's *Uncle Tom's Cabin*."[130]

Evangelicals in Great Britain led the first large campaign in history. The first wave was in 1783/1787/1788. In 1807 its successes set in. The second wave came in 1791/1792, and the successes of the second wave arose in 1833. It resembles present day campaigns by Amnesty International, for example, and it was demonstrated here for the first time how a

---

[126] Hochgeschwender. *Religion*, pp. 102-103, see all of pp. 101-104.
[127] Egon Flaig. *Weltgeschichte der Sklaverei*. München: C. H. Beck, 2009, p. 199 (chapter 8).
[128] Alvin J. Schmidt. *Wie das Christentum die Welt veränderte*. op. cit., pp. 330-344.
[129] Jochen Meissner et. al. *Schwarzes Amerika*. op. cit., pp. 198, see also p. 202.
[130] Jochen Meissner et. al. *Schwarzes Amerika*. op. cit., p. 202.

political minority without influence can assert its human rights concerns through mobilizing a population. At first they collected almost 400,000 signatures for the second campaign, and then 750,000 to 1,275,000 signatures. This was respectively 1/5 and 1/3 of all those who were able to sign. This is due to the fact that there were about 4 million men under 16 years of age.[131] The sugar campaign also became well-known after a book by William Fox, which struck large segments of the population.[132] All of this was led by innumerable local committees[133], in which Evangelical women above all played a role.[134]

William Wilberforce had been a representative in the British House of Commons since 1780. He converted to Evangelical Protestantism in 1784 on a trip through continental Europe and founded the *Abolition Society* in order to elevate morals and especially abolish the slave trade. In a parliamentary meeting in 1789, Wilberforce, along with William Pitt, petitioned for the first time in the House of Commons to abolish the slave trade. Again in 1792 a petition was filed, this time successfully. Yet implementation was prevented due to war and the situation in the colonies. It was not until 1807 that an act of Parliament ended the British slave trade. Slave traders within the British sphere of control were viewed as pirates and punished. The United States of America followed, whereby beginning in 1808 the slave trade was forbidden.

At that point Wilberforce set his sights on implementing this prohibition in the rest of the civilized world. Upon his urging, Lord Castlereagh successfully raised this as an issue at the Congress of Vienna. Finally, there were agreements in which France, Spain, and Portugal obligated themselves to forbid the slave trade

After the slave trade was abolished, Wilberforce finally became active in ostracizing and eliminating slavery itself. In 1816 he presented a motion in Parliament to reduce the number of slaves in the British West Indies. The government began preparing the emancipation of all slaves in 1823, and Wilberforce held impassioned speeches throughout the fierce debate until in 1825, he had to retire due to health reasons. He died in 1833 and was buried in the church of the British crown, Westminster Abbey.

---

[131] Seymour Drescher. *Abolition*. op. cit., pp. 202, 209, 220, 229.
[132] J. R. Oldfield. *Popular Politics and British Anti-Slavery*. op. cit., p. 57; Seymour Drescher. *Abolition*. op. cit., p. 201.
[133] J. R. Oldfield. *Popular Politics and British Anti-Slavery*. op. cit., Pp. 96-124.
[134] Oldfield, p. 141.

Next to all the moral considerations, slavery was also not a profitable contributor to the economy; rather, in economic terms it produced a loss. If slaves had been replaced by oxen, tools and a feudal levy system at the time that sugar cane plantations sprang up, the revenues and the profits would have been much higher.[135] Slaves could not earn anything. Any additional effort was pointless, and thinking for themselves was of no benefit. Rather, in the best case, it was only of value to the master. "During all of human history, slaves' passivity always led to the downfall of the system that made use of their services."[136]

"In 1776 the abolitionists received additional support from an unexpected direction – from a standard work of economics, Adam Smith's *The Wealth of Nations*. Smith came to the conclusion that slavery was uneconomical, on the one hand due to the fact that it ruined the country, and on the other because the subsistence of slaves was more expensive than that for a free worker. However, he made it clear to which basis slavery, according to his own conviction, could be traced back: 'The pride of mankind misguides man to enjoy domination ... he will generally prefer the services of a slave to the services of a free man.'"[137]

The American South, with its slave-based society, was poor when viewed as a whole in contrast to the slave-free American North. However, the fact cannot be hidden that some slave and plantation owners wallowed in wealth.[138] This should, however, not lead to the assumption that slavery was abolished because it was already in the grips of demise. More recent research shows that slavery was at a highpoint with respect to its profitability for those participating in it and that the number of transported and engaged slaves was higher than ever before. Additionally, slavery was abolished at the time when British pride was at its highest level.[139]

More recent authors are correct that the abolition of slavery was above all forced through by moral purists (whom we might today call 'fundamentalists'[140]) to whom the continually stated economic conse-

---

[135] Details in Henry Hobhouse. *Fünf Pflanzen verändern die Welt.* dtv: Frankfurt, 1987, p. 97; comp. the concrete calculations for a sugar plantation in Susanne Everett. *Geschichte der Sklaverei.* Bechtermünz Verlag: Augsburg, 1998, pp. 74-75.
[136] Henry Hobhouse. *Fünf Pflanzen verändern die Welt.* op. cit., p. 233.
[137] Susanne Everett. *Geschichte der Sklaverei.* Bechtermünz Verlag: Augsburg, 1998, p. 137.
[138] Comp. ibid., pp. 233-235.
[139] So in particular Seymour Drescher. *Abolition.* op. cit., p. 121.
[140] Comp.Thomas Schirrmacher. *Fundamentalism: When Religion becomes Dangerous.* Bonn: VKW, 2013.

quences did not matter when compared to the human dignity of those affected by slavery.[141] The French Revolution left slavery in the colonies untouched and put down uprisings by slaves. Thus the Enlightenment did not make any significant contribution to the abolition of slavery.[142]

In 1975 Roger Anstey defended and documented the thesis that Evangelicals were so strongly opposed to slavery because they understood conversion and redemption to be from the slavery of sin into the freedom of the gospel, and for that reason could only view slavery negatively.[143] The fight against slavery was an "end in itself"[144] for Evangelicals and a moral truth that could not be surrendered. For this reason it neither impressed them that they actually did not have any political power, nor that the abolition of the slave trade would have alleged or actual grave consequences for the economy.

Christopher Leslie Brown writes in his monumental history of the abolition of slavery, *Moral Capital* (2006), that the role of Evangelicals has been blocked out and indeed at times renounced since the last comprehensive investigation written by Roger Anstey in 1975.[145] Seymour Drescher is of the same opinion in his monumental history of the anti-slavery movement,[146] whereby he additionally points out that the role of William Wilberforce has especially been suppressed.

This is due to the fact, among others, that from about 1975-2000 one above all saw the abolition of slavery accounted for in economic and social terms. It was not until most recent times that a differing opinion on the part of researchers gained the upper hand. That opinion says that slavery was abolished at the time of its high point, that without the anti-slavery movement it would have still been able to continue for a long time, and that the decisive reasons were not primarily economic but rather coming from intellectual history.[147] Additionally, Christopher Leslie Brown points out – and this might astound many today – that Evangelical women played a central role in the anti-slavery movement. This is be-

---

[141] So also Seymour Drescher. *Abolition.* op. cit., pp. 331, 205-206.
[142] So also Seymour Drescher. *Abolition.* op. cit., pp. 161-165; Jochen Meissner et. al. *Schwarzes Amerika.* op. cit.
[143] Roger Anstey. *The Atlantic Slave Trade and British Abolition 1760-1810.* op. cit., pp. 157-183 "The Evangelical World View"; this is affirmed by Christopher Leslie Brown. *Moral Capital.* op. cit., pp. 336.
[144] Christopher Leslie Brown. *Moral Capital.* op. cit., p. 388.
[145] Roger Anstey. The Atlantic Slave Trade and British Abolition 1760-1810. op. cit.
[146] Seymour Drescher. Abolition. op. cit., pp. 377-380, 335-337; comp. the literature also with John Wolffe. *The Expansion of Evangelicalism.* op. cit., pp. 195-196.
[147] So for instance also Jochen Meissner et. al. *Schwarzes Amerika.* op. cit., p. 174.

cause it was an uprising of lay people and not of ecclesiastical or political office holders.[148]

William Gervase Clarence-Smith has depicted how the great religions of the world stood in reference to the abolition of slavery.[149] The first large scale rejection was found in the Protestant world. In terms of the Catholic side, there were repeatedly popes who turned against slave trading in other individuals, but even in the papal states there were slaves. It was not until 1839 that Pope Gregory VI turned against the trading of slaves (not yet against slavery in itself). And it was not until 1888, when Brazil as the final Catholic country abolished slavery, that Pope Leo XIII turned against slavery itself and did this by condemning Islamic slavery.[150] Orthodox churches needed even longer.[151]

In Buddhism (as in most Eastern religions), there was as in Christianity predominantly an early shift from slavery to serfdom. More official Buddhist rejections of slavery only began in the 19th century.[152]

10. Slavery in the Islamic World

Without wanting to downplay slavery by Europeans, it has to be pointed out that slavery within the realm of Islam was vastly more brutal than "Christian" slavery. "The largest slave traders and owners of slaves in history were the Arabs."[153] On account of better treatment, many descendants of European slaves, however, survived, while the slaves of Islamic peoples were seldom able to increase and thus perished. The result is that today, as a result of descendants of slaves in the "Christian" world, there is the impression that practically only western peoples held slaves.[154] Tidiane N'Diaye writes: "While the transatlantic slave trade lasted four hundred years, Arabs plundered the African continent south of the Sahara for thirteen hundred years. The largest portion of the millions

---

[148]   Christopher Leslie Brown. *Moral Capital*. op. cit., p. 343ff.

[149]   William Gervase Clarence-Smith. *Islam and the Abolition of Slavery*. Oxford/New York: Oxford University Press, 2006, pp. 219-234.

[150]   Ibid., pp. 223-227.

[151]   Ibid., pp. 227-228.

[152]   Ibid., p. 229ff.

[153]   Walter Krämer, Götz Trenkler. *Lexikon der populären Irrtümer*. Eichborn: Frankfurt, 1997[12], p. 288 (with literature references).

[154]   Vgl. Walter Krämer, Götz Trenkler. *Lexikon der populären Irrtümer*. op. cit., p. 289.

of deported Africans died as a consequence of inhumane treatment and systematically used castration."[155]

That Islamic slavery was worse than the European model is above all brought forward by Egon Flaig in his *Weltgeschichte der Sklaverei* (*World History of Slavery*)[156] and from an African point of view by Tidiane N'Diaye.[157] Egon Flaig writes: "When Muslims seized their world empire, they erected the largest and longest lasting system of slavery in world history. Islamic slavery has been glossed over since the 19th century."[158]

"This first world economic system – as the largest system of slavery in world history – called for a steady and enormous influx of slaves. It was also for this reason that permanently fighting wars and incessantly attacking non-Muslim neighbors was of decisive importance."[159]

"In the process, slavery in antiquity was not prominent from a quantitative point of view. The Islamic form was the most comprehensive in history; the transatlantic form is significant because from the beginning it was opposed and because its political and in part violent abolition was the lever for defeating it around the world."[160]

Tidiane N'Diaye writes in a similar vein: "While the transatlantic slave trade lasted from the 16th to the 19th century, Arab Muslims plundered black people groups from the 7th up into the 20th century. For almost ten centuries they even possessed the monopoly in this ignominious business and thereby deported almost ten million Africans. It was not until then that Europeans appeared, since the black continent had only been known to them since the return of Vasco de Gama from India in 1499. Thus the arrival of the Arabs, who were in Africa long before the Europeans, did not provide the kick-off to 'one hundred years of isolation' for black peoples but rather to 'one thousand years of martyrdom.'"[161]

---

[155] Tidiane N'Diaye. *Der verschleierte Völkermord: Die Geschichte des muslimischen Sklavenhandels in Afrika.* Reinbek bei Hamburg: Rowohlt, 2010, p. 12.
[156] Egon Flaig. *Weltgeschichte der Sklaverei.* op. cit.; comp. additionally William Gervase Clarence-Smith. *Islam and the Abolition of Slavery.* op. cit.; Klaus Hock. "Jihad – Mahaismus – Sklaverei. Eine islamische Tradition der Gewalt im Zentralsudan?" pp. 67-78 in: Ulrich Van der Heyden, Jürgen Becher. *Mission und Gewalt. Missionsgeschichtliches Archiv 6.* Stuttgart: Franz Steiner, 2000.
[157] Tidiane N'Diaye. *Der verschleierte Völkermord.* op. cit.; comp. with the book by N'Diaye: Ulrich Baron. "Als muslimische Sklavenjäger Afrika entvölkerten: Verschleierter Völkermord." *Die Welt* dated March 30,.2010. p. 23.
[158] Egon Flaig. *Weltgeschichte der Sklaverei.* op. cit., p. 83.
[159] Egon Flaig. *Weltgeschichte der Sklaverei.* op. cit., p. 87.
[160] Egon Flaig. *Weltgeschichte der Sklaverei.* op. cit., p. 11.
[161] Tidiane N'Diaye. *Der verschleierte Völkermord.* op. cit., p. 211.

"Millions of Africans were attacked, massacred, taken captive, or castrated and taken under inhumane conditions through the Sahara in caravans or deported from east African trading posts for human commodities via the sea route to the Arab-Islamic world."[162]

"Long before the Europeans entered into the business of slavery, Arabs conducted an endless holy war with bloody raids, which for the sake of the splendor of the Oriental harem brought disaster to complete people groups, men, women, and children from the heart of the black continent."[163]

In the process, it was not only a question of the enslavement of Africans – which was bad enough – but rather a question also relating directly to the enslavement of Europeans. This was part of the reason for Europe's panic when the Turks stood before Vienna. For example, from 1580-1680 there were 7,000 Europeans enslaved every day and carried off to the Maghreb states.[164]

Additionally, it has to be said that a centuries long theological discussion for and against slavery such as occurred in Christianity never took place in the Islamic world.[165] This is shown in the most comprehensive history of the abolition of slavery in the Islamic world.[166] Tidiane N'Diaye summarizes it: "Simply stated, in the Arab-Islamic world a tradition of critique or even of self-criticism has simply been always missing, especially when it has to do with non-refuted practices of Islam."[167] "One wonders, however, why innumerable authors become fixated on ignoring this and limit their research to the slave trade that was once conducted by western nations?"[168]

Western authors predominantly treat the history of Islamic slavery with a velvet glove, and the topic is simply ignored by Muslim authors. Muslims have long denounced Christian slavery, but they forget to mention their own. As an example, William Gervase Clarence-Smith mentions Hamdan ben Uthman Khoja in the year 1833.[169] At the World Muslim

---

[162] Tidiane N'Diaye. *Der verschleierte Völkermord.* op. cit., p. 11.

[163] Tidiane N'Diaye. *Der verschleierte Völkermord.* op. cit., p. 25.

[164] Egon Flaig. *Weltgeschichte der Sklaverei.* op. cit., p. 28.

[165] Egon Flaig. *Weltgeschichte der Sklaverei.* op. cit., p. 199.

[166] William Gervase Clarence-Smith. *Islam and the Abolition of Slavery.* op. cit.

[167] Tidiane N'Diaye. *Der verschleierte Völkermord.* op. cit., p. 203. On the extreme seldom voices, in particular of Islamic minorities or splinter groups in England in the late 18th century and then in particular since the 1870s comp. William Gervase Clarence-Smith. *Islam and the Abolition of Slavery.* op. cit., pp. 232-234.

[168] Tidiane N'Diaye. *Der verschleierte Völkermord.* op. cit., p. 199.

[169] William Gervase Clarence-Smith. *Islam and the Abolition of Slavery.* op. cit., p. 1.

Congress in Mogadishu in 1964-1965, 33 Islamic countries maintained that they could not have fellowship with countries which operate imperialistically and conduct slavery, since these are un-Islamic. However, in this connection they only mentioned western countries and ignored their own, Islamic examples.[170] At the UN anti-racism conference in Durban, it was of all people the Justice Minister of Sudan who amid applause from other Islamic states called for reparations from the west for the time of slavery, although Sudan is supposedly that country on the globe where slavery is most widespread.[171] "As early as 1996 the special envoy of the United Nations to Sudan pointed to a 'terrifying increase in slavery, the slave trade, and forced labor in Sudan.'"[172]

11. Slavery and Human Trafficking today

Since slavery still exists,[173] even if is forbidden almost everywhere, the Old and New Testament ban against hunting for slaves, upon the threat of the highest form of punishment, is still a current topic. Forbidding slavery occurred recently in Saudi Arabia, in 1962, and in Oman in 1970.[174]

Today slavery means to force someone to work by using physical or psychological force or by threat, and thereby to treat and trade that individual as a possession and to restrict that individual's free movement, even if lawful possession is avoided. A widespread, brutal form of debt

---

[170] Ibid., pp. 1-2 with reference to *The Islamic Review* 53 (1965): 27-29.
[171] According to Egon Flaig. *Weltgeschichte der Sklaverei*. op. cit., pp. 215-216.
[172] Tidiane N'Diaye. *Der verschleierte Völkermord*. op. cit., p. 13.
[173] Comp. in part. Kevin Bales, Zoe Trodd, Alex Kent Williamson. *Modern Slavery*. Oneworld: Oxford, 2009; Kevin Bales, Becky Cornell. *Moderne Sklaverei*. Hildesheim: Gerstenberg, 2008; *Jahrbuch Menschenrechte 2008: Schwerpunkt: Sklaverei heute*. Frankfurt: Suhrkamp, 2007; E. Benjamin Skinner. *Menschenhandel: Sklaverei im 21. Jahrhundert*. Bergisch Gladbach: Gustav Lübbe, 2008 (12 countries' reports and destinies); Mike Kaye. *Arrested Development: Discrimination and Slavery in the 21st Century*. London: Anti-Slavery International, 2008, many reposts at www.antislavery.org/english/resources/reports/default.aspx; Krishna Prasad Upadhyaya. *Poverty, Discrimination and Slavery: The Reality of bonded Labour in India, Nepal and Pakistan*. London: Anti-Slavery International, 2008, www.antislavery.org/homepage/resources/PDF/PDFbondedlabour.htm; Roger Sawyer. *Slavery in the Twentieth Century*. Routledge & Kegan Paul: London, 1986; Sonderseite "Moderne Sklaverei." *Die Welt* dated December 8, 1999, p. 6; Dietrich Alexander. "Sudan – wo die Freiheit eines Menschen 50 Dollar wert ist." *Die Welt* dated December 8, 1999, p. 6.
[174] As in David Brion Davis. *Slavery and Human Progress*. Oxford University Press: New York (NY), 1984, p. 317.

servanthood, by which families incur larger debts with their employers for means of labour than they receive as payment, is the most widespread form of slavery and particularly affects many children.[175] (As mentioned, this is something different from the debt servanthood in the Old Testament, by which actual debts were worked off in instalments.)

The reasons for slavery are, according to Kevin Bales: easier profit, missing or ineffective punishment, poverty, restrictive immigration laws, missing information on those affected. Globally there is USD $32 billion profit made on trafficking people, and slavery generates income that totals USD $42 billion.[176]

Differences between old and new slavery[177]	
Not globalized	Globalized
Legal possession	Legal and illegal possession avoided
Long-term relationship	Short-term relationship
Racial differences important	Racial differences less important
High purchase price	Low purchase price
Low profit	High profit
Scant number of potential slaves	Abundant number of potential slaves
Slaves held for a long time	Slaves can be exchanged at any time

The oldest human rights organization in the world, the British organization Anti-Slavery International, uses a broad definition of slavery and reckons that there are 100 million slaves worldwide.[178] (For sake of contrast, one should recall the estimate that between 1450 and 1900, 11.7 million people from Africa were enslaved, of whom 9.8 million arrived in

---

[175] See *Kinderarbeit in der Welt* (Bericht der Bundesregierung). Bundesministerium für Arbeit und Sozialordnung: Bonn, 1995, pp. 30-34.

[176] Alles Kevin Bales, Zoe Trodd, Alex Kent Williamson. *Modern Slavery*. op. cit., pp. 43-44 and often.

[177] Nach Kevin Bales, Zoe Trodd, Alex Kent Williamson. *Modern Slavery*. op. cit., p. 28.

[178] "Slavery." *Newsweek* dated May 4, 1992, pp. 8-16, here p. 8; comp. the similar numbers of the UN's International Labour Organisation (www.ilo.org), see in part. "Kinderarbeit: Eine Schande für die Menschheit." ILO-Spezial. International Labour Organization, Vertretung Bonn, Bonn o. J. (approx. 1998), pp. 1-4.

the country of destination.[179]) The leading researcher with respect to present day slavery, Kevin Bales, uses a very precise definition of slavery and comes to a number of 27 million slaves worldwide, which is more than at any time in history and more were carried off and enslaved in the past 350 years of history.[180] Slavery today, since it is illegal everywhere, is more or less hidden but can be detected without much effort.

According to studies by Bales and others, there are 20 million slaves in South Asia, of which 10 million are in India, namely in households, in forced marriages, in forced prostitution and in debt servanthood. In the latter they are primarily in brickworks, in rice mills, and in agriculture.[181] In addition, there is primarily slavery in Southeast Asia and North and western Africa.

80 % of slaves are privately held, and 20% are held by government institutions or armies involved in civil wars. 8.4 million slaves are children, of which 5.7 million work, 1.8 million are ensnared in prostitution and pornography, 0.6 million are in gangs committing petty crimes, 0.3 million are child soldiers. Globally, 1.2 million have been abducted. Thousands of boys from Pakistan, Bangladesh, Sudan and Mauritania have been taken to the Arab Emirates to be camel jockeys. In Haiti poor families send their children to rich families, where they often work 14 hours per day in a household and are frequently abused. The government estimates the number at 90,000-120,000, ILO 250,000, and UNICEF 300,000. In Pakistan 500,000 child slaves work in the rug industry, and in India the number is 300,000.

In the USA there are 40,000 slaves, of which 49% are in the sex industry, 27% work in households, and 10% in agriculture. According to the government in the USA, between 14,000 and 17,000 slaves are abducted annually.[182]

The Lagogai Research Foundation assumes that in China there are 1 million people who are under forced labor in 1,045 camps, and ILO sets the number at 260,000.[183]

---

[179]   According to Henry Hobhouse. *Fünf Pflanzen verändern die Welt*. dtv: Frankfurt, 1987, p. 93 (without losses in Africa).
[180]   Z. B. Kevin Bales, Zoe Trodd, Alex Kent Williamson. *Modern Slavery*. op. cit., p. vii.
[181]   On India see *Poverty, Discrimination and Slavery: The Reality of bonded Labour in India, Nepal and Pakistan*. Krishna Prasad Upadhyaya Anti-Slavery International 2008. http://www.antislavery.org/includes/documents/cm_docs/2009/p/1_povertyd iscriminationslaveryfinal.pdf.
[182]   Everything from Kevin Bales, Zoe Trodd, Alex Kent Williamson. *Modern Slavery*. op. cit., pp. 18-23.
[183]   Ibid., p. 103.

800,000 people are traded across national borders annually, of which 80% are women, In turn, 50% of them are children.[184] No continent is excluded, Europe as well![185]

Ironically, some of the worst slavery is found in the Dominican Republic among Haitians, although this is the only country in which African slaves were successful in taking over the government. Approximately one million slaves still work there on the sugar plantations.

A 1981 UN Report[186] estimated the number of slaves in Mauritania at 100,000. Here one is dealing with the question of slaves who are abducted. This is to say that it has to do with a type of slavery that was most sharply condemned in the Old Testament, where it carried the threat of capital punishment. However, nothing has changed in Mauritania since that time. In addition to Mauritania, one can mention Kuwait, where slavery is primarily known though Kuwaitis in London. There, slaves have escaped and informed the police.[187] Ironically, in the First Gulf War the UN, and in particular the USA, acted to defend and maintain a society that holds slaves.[188] Slavery in Africa and in Islamic countries in Northern Africa was indeed strongly curtailed in the 1960s, but it flourished around the Sahara, namely in Mauritania, Mali, Niger, Sudan, and Chad as it had before, whereby the owners were mostly Muslim Arabs and the slaves mostly black.[189] In Niger, Mauritania, Mali, and other areas of West Africa there is

---

[184] Ibid., p. 36.

[185] See *Begging for Change: Research findings and recommendations on forced child begging in Albania/Greece, India and Senegal* Emily Delap Anti-Slavery International 2009 http://www.antislavery.org/includes/documents/cm_docs/2009/b/beggingforc hange09.pdf and on Great Britain: *Missing Out: A Study of Child Trafficking in the North-West, North-East and West Midlands* The report highlights the cases of 80 children known or suspected of being trafficked into the UK for sexual exploitation, labour exploitation and forced marriage. More shocking is that 48 of these children have gone missing from social services care and have never been found. Christine Beddoe, ECPAT UK, 2007 http://www.ecpat.org.uk/downloads/ECPAT_ UK_Missing_Out_2007.pdf.

[186] Bernard D. Nossiter. "U. N. Group Gets Report on Slaves in Mauritania." New York Times dated August 21, 1981; comp. Roger Sawyer. *Slavery in the Twentieth Century*. op. cit., pp. 14 and "Slavery," Newsweek dated May 4, 1992, pp. 8-16, here pp. 9-12.

[187] "Slavery," *Newsweek* dated May 4. 1992, pp. 8-16, here pp. 12-13.

[188] On the situation of female slaves in the Near East see *Trafficking in Women, Forced Labour and Domestic Work: in the context of the Middle East and Gulf Region*. Anti-Slavery International 2008 2006 http://www.antislavery.org/includes/docu ments/cm_docs/2009/t/traffic_women_forced_labour_domestic_2006.pdf.

[189] David Brion Davis. *Slavery and Human Progress*. op. cit., p. 319.

still slavery from birth, which means that the offspring of slaves are automatically counted as slaves and as children are already forced into slave labour.

In addition, comprehensive slavery enables prostitution. Global, cruel trafficking in girls is the most widespread form of modern slavery,[190] yet with the global growth in homosexuality there are increasingly more boys who fall into the trap of the slave mill in spite of all the propaganda to the contrary. It is a matter of millions of child prostitutes. And the sex tourism that is enabled through this slavery is becoming an increasingly important component of Western tourism and source of foreign currency for countries in the Third World. According to Will Durant, Ancient Greece experienced its downfall through a combination of sexual exploitation and slavery,[191] and Western Civilization is well on the way to repeating this.

According to Amnesty International, 500,000 young girls are abducted to Europe.[192] In Thailand,[193] Brazil, and India[194] it is primarily children who are enslaved, with many of them in the prostitution trade.[195]

Trafficking African women in Europe – according to comprehensive studies of two Austrian researchers – rests in the hands of pimps (*madames*), predominantly themselves former slaves.[196] In front of the Vienna trade fair grounds everyone can see long rows of black girls and women

[190] See above all Mary Kreutzer, Corinna Milborn. *Ware Frau: Auf den Spuren moderner Sklaverei von Afrika nach Europa.* Ecowin: Salzburg, 2008; Jürgen Nautz, Birgit Sauer (eds.). *Frauenhandel. Transkulturelle Perspektiven 6.* V&R unipress: Göttingen, 2008 (Austria and East Europe); Ernesto Savona, Sonia Stefanizzi (eds.). *Measuring Human Trafficking.* Spirnger: Berlin, 2007 (on the problematic nature of reliable numbers); Heinz G. Schmidt. *Der neue Sklavenmarkt: Geschäfte mit Frauen in Übersee.* Lenos-Verlag: Basel, 1985; Regula Renschler et al. (eds.). *Ware Liebe: Sextourismus-Prostitution-Frauenhandel.* Peter Hammer Verlag: Wuppertal, 1988²; Regina Kalthegener. "Zwangsprostitution," pp. 88-97 in: *Jahrbuch Menschenrechte 2008: Schwerpunkt: Sklaverei heute.* Frankfurt: Suhrkamp, 2007.
[191] Will Durant. *The Life of Greece.* Simon and Schuster: New York, 1939, pp. 562-568.
[192] Mary Kreutzer, Corinna Milborn. *Ware Frau.* op. cit., pp. 9, 38.
[193] ccording to "Kinderarbeit: Eine Schande für die Menschheit." ILO-Spezial. International Labour Organization, Vertretung Bonn, Bonn o. J. (approx. 1998). Pp. 1-4 in Thailand 160,000 children under 16 work in the prostitution trade, increasingly boys.
[194] Comp. on India Swapan Kumar Sinha. *Child Labour in Calcutta: A Sociological Study.* Naya Prokash: Calcutta, 1991.
[195] See Karl-Ludwig Günsche. "Die moderne Form der Sklaverei: Unicef prangert sexuelle Ausbeutung von Kindern an." *Die Welt* dated August 22, 1996. p. 2.
[196] Mary Kreutzer, Corinna Milborn. *Ware Frau.* op. cit., pp. 9, 45, 48.

from Nigeria. The method is as follows: women pay large amounts for rent, food, and clothing which they are unable to repay. The best pressure is thereby a "pact with the family at home in Africa,"[197] and "the most effective means ... are magic rituals."[198] A true interest on the part of the authorities to dry up this type of slavery cannot be detected by researchers: "Only all too often the state plays into the hands of the human traffickers."[199] "It is strange that after several months of research we were able to identify the madams, while the police apparently were groping in the dark."[200]

The customers remain completely unchecked, whereas actually there should be legislation, criminal prosecution, and prevention. "The market produces trafficking in women."[201] "Without customers who are indifferent to the destiny of women whom they rent, there would be no forced prostitution and no trafficking in women."[202] After surveying customers, researchers come to the conclusion: "That trafficking in women is a basis for street walking is something that whoremongers know.[203]

The African Nobel Prize winner in literature, Wole Soyinka, gives as an example the system in Ghana disclosed by the CNN journalist Christiane Amanpour, according to which a girl has to live as a bride of the gods and as a slave of a priest until she is no longer beautiful. The priest owes her nothing, and she owes him everything. In the process rape is the rule.[204]

The Old and New Testaments did not totally outlaw slavery in all circumstances, but the comprehensive provisions for the legal protection of servants and maidservants, as well as the right to be redeemed through the use of a slaves' own possessions or by others, fundamentally distinguishes the slavery that is described there from the later slavery of the 15th to the 18th centuries and from the present day, illegal slavery that occurs everywhere. *It is no wonder that in spite of all the twists and errors within Christianity, the thought established itself that God was completely against modern slavery and that all slaves should be set free.*

---

[197] Ibid., p. 51.
[198] Ibid., p. 52.
[199] Ibid., p. 155.
[200] Ibid., p. 48.
[201] Ibid., p. 214.
[202] Ibid., p. 59.
[203] Ibid., p. 75.
[204] Wole Soyinka. "Kulturelle Ansprüche und globale Rechte." pp. 45-58 in: *Versprochen – Verletzt – Gefordert: 50 Jahre Allgemeine Erklärung der Menschenrechte*. Forum Menschenrechte Materialien 12. Forum Menschenrechte: Bonn, 1998, here pp. 45-46.

World Evangelical Alliance

World Evangelical Alliance is a global ministry working with local churches around the world to join in common concern to live and proclaim the Good News of Jesus in their communities. WEA is a network of churches in 129 nations that have each formed an evangelical alliance and over 100 international organizations joining together to give a worldwide identity, voice and platform to more than 600 million evangelical Christians. Seeking holiness, justice and renewal at every level of society – individual, family, community and culture, God is glorified and the nations of the earth are forever transformed.

Christians from ten countries met in London in 1846 for the purpose of launching, in their own words, "a new thing in church history, a definite organization for the expression of unity amongst Christian individuals belonging to different churches." This was the beginning of a vision that was fulfilled in 1951 when believers from 21 countries officially formed the World Evangelical Fellowship. Today, 150 years after the London gathering, WEA is a dynamic global structure for unity and action that embraces 600 million evangelicals in 129 countries. It is a unity based on the historic Christian faith expressed in the evangelical tradition. And it looks to the future with vision to accomplish God's purposes in discipling the nations for Jesus Christ.

Commissions:

- Theology
- Missions
- Religious Liberty
- Women's Concerns
- Youth
- Information Technology

Initiatives and Activities

- Ambassador for Human Rights
- Ambassador for Refugees
- Creation Care Task Force
- Global Generosity Network
- International Institute for Religious Freedom
- International Institute for Islamic Studies
- Leadership Institute
- Micah Challenge
- Global Human Trafficking Task Force
- Peace and Reconciliation Initiative
- UN-Team

Church Street Station
P.O. Box 3402
New York, NY 10008-3402
Phone +[1] 212 233 3046
Fax +[1] 646-957-9218
www.worldea.org

Giving Hands

GIVING HANDS GERMANY (GH) was established in 1995 and is officially recognized as a nonprofit foreign aid organization. It is an international operating charity that – up to now – has been supporting projects in about 40 countries on four continents. In particular we care for orphans and street children. Our major focus is on Africa and Central America. GIVING HANDS always mainly provides assistance for self-help and furthers human rights thinking.

The charity itself is not bound to any church, but on the spot we are co-operating with churches of all denominations. Naturally we also cooperate with other charities as well as governmental organizations to provide assistance as effective as possible under the given circumstances.

The work of GIVING HANDS GERMANY is controlled by a supervisory board. Members of this board are Manfred Feldmann, Colonel V. Doner and Kathleen McCall. Dr. Christine Schirrmacher is registered as legal manager of GIVING HANDS at the local district court. The local office and work of the charity are coordinated by Rev. Horst J. Kreie as executive manager. Dr. theol. Thomas Schirrmacher serves as a special consultant for all projects.

Thanks to our international contacts companies and organizations from many countries time and again provide containers with gifts in kind which we send to the different destinations where these goods help to satisfy elementary needs. This statutory purpose is put into practice by granting nutrition, clothing, education, construction and maintenance of training centers at home and abroad, construction of wells and operation of water treatment systems, guidance for self-help and transportation of goods and gifts to areas and countries where needy people live.

GIVING HANDS has a publishing arm under the leadership of Titus Vogt, that publishes human rights and other books in English, Spanish, Swahili and other languages.

These aims are aspired to the glory of the Lord according to the basic Christian principles put down in the Holy Bible.

Baumschulallee 3a • D-53115 Bonn • Germany
Phone: +49 / 228 / 695531 • Fax +49 / 228 / 695532
www.gebende-haende.de • info@gebende-haende.de

Martin Bucer Seminary

Faithful to biblical truth
Cooperating with the Evangelical Alliance
Reformed

Solid training for the Kingdom of God
- Alternative theological education
- Study while serving a church or working another job
- Enables students to remain in their own churches
- Encourages independent thinking
- Learning from the growth of the universal church.

Academic
- For the Bachelor's degree: 180 Bologna-Credits
- For the Master's degree: 120 additional Credits
- Both old and new teaching methods: All day seminars, independent study, term papers, etc.

Our Orientation:
- Complete trust in the reliability of the Bible
- Building on reformation theology
- Based on the confession of the German Evangelical Alliance
- Open for innovations in the Kingdom of God

Our Emphasis:
- The Bible
- Ethics and Basic Theology
- Missions
- The Church

Our Style:
- Innovative
- Relevant to society
- International
- Research oriented
- Interdisciplinary

Structure
- 15 study centers in 7 countries with local partners
- 5 research institutes
- President: Prof. Dr. Thomas Schirrmacher
  Vice President: Prof. Dr. Thomas K. Johnson
- Deans: Thomas Kinker, Th.D.;
  Titus Vogt, lic. theol., Carsten Friedrich, M.Th.

Missions through research
- Institute for Religious Freedom
- Institute for Islamic Studies
- Institute for Life and Family Studies
- Institute for Crisis, Dying, and Grief Counseling
- Institute for Pastoral Care

www.bucer.eu • info@bucer.eu

Berlin | Bielefeld | Bonn | Chemnitz | Hamburg | Munich | Pforzheim
Innsbruck | Istanbul | Izmir | Linz | Prague | São Paulo | Tirana | Zurich

Made in the USA
Coppell, TX
01 August 2022